GUINNESS WORLD RECORDS

GUINNESS WORLD RECORDS

EXTREME

Compiled by Lisa L. Ryan-Herndon

For Guinness World Records:
Laura Barrett Plunkett, Craig Glenday and Stuart Claxton

D1468323

■SCHOLASTIC

New York • Toronto • London • Auckland • Sydney
Mexico City • New Delhi • Hong Kong • Buenos Aires • Puerto Rico

ATTEMPTING TO BREAK RECORDS OR SET NEW RECORDS CAN BE DANGEROUS. APPROPRIATE ADVICE SHOULD BE TAKEN FIRST, AND ALL RECORD ATTEMPTS ARE UNDERTAKEN ENTIRELY AT THE PARTICIPANT'S RISK. IN NO CIRCUMSTANCES WILL GUINNESS WORLD RECORDS LIMITED OR SCHOLASTIC HAVE ANY LIABILITY FOR DEATH OR INJURY SUFFERED IN ANY RECORD ATTEMPTS. GUINNESS WORLD RECORDS LIMITED HAS COMPLETE DISCRETION OVER WHETHER OR NOT TO INCLUDE ANY PARTICULAR RECORDS IN THE ANNUAL GUINNESS WORLD RECORDS BOOK.

© 2007 Guinness World Records Limited, a HIT Entertainment Limited Company.

SCHOLASTIC
Published by Scholastic Australia Pty Limited
ABN 11 000 614 577
PO Box 579 Gosford NSW 2250
www.scholastic.com.au

Part of the Scholastic Group
Sydney · Auckland · New York · Toronto · London · Mexico City
New Delhi · Hong Kong · Buenos Aires · Puerto Rico

ISBN 978-1-74169-027-9

Photo research by Els Rijper.
Records from the Archives of Guinness World Records.
This edition designed by Simone Kelleher.
Printed by Leo Paper Group, Hong Kong.

10 9 8 7 6 5 4 3 2 1   7 8 9 / 0

Visit Guinness World Records at **www.guinnessworldrecords.com**

CONTENTS

A RECORD-BREAKING HISTORY 4

TO THE EXTREME! 5

EXTREME SKILLS 6

EXTREME KILLERS 18

EXTREME DANGER 28

EXTREME SPEED 36

EXTREME ON THE MOVE 44

EXTREME SOUNDS 52

EXTREME SMELLS 60

EXTREME EXTENSIONS 68

EXTREME TEETH 80

EXTREME FOOD 88

EXTREME LUXURIES 96

EXTREME APPETITES 108

EXTREME SURVIVORS 118

EXTREME-ISTS 126

BE A RECORD-BREAKER! 137

QUIZZED OUT! 138

CONCLUSION 141

PHOTO CREDITS 142

A RECORD-BREAKING HISTORY

The idea for Guinness World Records grew out of a question. In 1951, Sir Hugh Beaver, the managing director of the Guinness Brewery, wanted to know which was the fastest game bird in Europe — the golden plover or the grouse? Some people argued that it was the grouse. Others claimed it was the plover. A book to settle the debate did not exist until Sir Hugh discovered the knowledgeable twin brothers Norris and Ross McWhirter, who lived in London.

Like their father and grandfather, the McWhirter twins loved information. They were just kids when they started clipping interesting facts from newspapers and memorising important dates in world history. As well as learning the names of every river, mountain range, and nation's capital, they knew the record for pole squatting (196 days in 1954), which language had only one irregular verb (Turkish), and that the grouse — flying at a timed speed of 70 kilometres per hour — is faster than the golden plover at 65 kilometres per hour.

Norris and Ross served in the British Royal Navy during World War II, graduated from university, and launched their own fact-finding business called McWhirter Twins Ltd. They were the perfect people to compile the book of records that Sir Hugh Beaver searched for yet could not find.

The first edition of *The Guinness Book of Records* was published on 27 August, 1955, and since then has been published in 37 languages and more than 100 countries. In 2000, the book title changed to *Guinness World Records* and has set an incredible record of its own: excluding non-copyrighted books such as the Bible and the Koran, *Guinness World Records* is the best-selling book of all time!

Today, the official Keeper of the Records keeps a careful eye on each Guinness World Record, compiling and verifying the greatest the world has to offer — from the fastest and the tallest to the slowest and the smallest, with everything in between.

TO THE EXTREME!

Can excellence be timed, measured and weighed?

Ask Guinness World Records, the leading authority in taking the measure of excellence in years and seconds, kilometres and centimetres, tonnes and grams — all for our information, astonishment and enjoyment.

For more than half a century, these official keepers of the records have tracked, documented and certified attempts made in every category, species and field imaginable. Today, over 40 000 fascinating facts and unforgettable achievements by people, animals, minerals, vegetables and mechanicals are stored inside their extensive archives.

This collection focuses on the sensational efforts of record-holders who went beyond the average and to the extreme in setting and breaking a Guinness World Record.

eXtreme SKILLS

Every day, record-breakers cross the line between ordinary and **eXTRAORDINARY.** These superstars perfected their skills and timing to exceed all expectations!

FASTEST SANDWICH MADE BY HUMAN FEET

It is considered good manners to wash up before dining. As the record-holder for **FASTEST SANDWICH MADE BY HUMAN FEET**, Rob Williams of Austin, Texas, USA, scrubs his toes and soles before and *after* picking up a fork and knife. Rob demonstrated his extraordinary sandwich-making skills during the TV show *Guinness World Records: Primetime* on 10 November, 2000. His adept toes stacked a cold meat-and-cheese sandwich in 1 minute 57 seconds — and he didn't hold the lettuce, tomatoes, or pickles!

'It's a pretty good sandwich, if you can get over the way it was created,' Rob claims. Anyone want a bite?

TRIVIA

A 'sole-full' sandwich has two slices of bread (taken out of the loaf packet in the time limit), cold meat (rind peeled off), slices of square processed cheese (plastic removed), lettuce, sliced tomatoes, mustard, mayonnaise and sliced pickles. Add olives on cocktail sticks, cut in half, then place on a plate!

MOST TOE WRESTLING WORLD CHAMPIONSHIP WINS

In 1976, the sport of toe wrestling pushed off at Ye Olde Royal Oak Inn located in Wetton, UK. Today, the sport has sprouted in popularity among all ages, and official toe inspectors eliminate prospective pushers if foot cleanliness is not up to snuff. Barefoot wrestlers lock toes and — on the command 'Toes away!' — attempt to 'toe-down' their opponent by forcing his or her toes across the specially constructed ring, known as a 'toe-rack'. The tip-top toe-curler takes the best of three matches.

The **MOST TOE WRESTLING WORLD CHAMPIONSHIP WINS** title for men belongs to five-time champion Alan 'Nasty' Nash of England. Alan won in 1994, 1996, 1997, 2000 and 2002. Karen Davies, also of England, holds the women's title as a four-time champion between 1999 and 2002.

TRIVIA

Alan's tough tootsies also earned the record for **MOST EGGS CRUSHED WITH THE TOES IN 30 SECONDS** with 23 eggs smashed on 11 September, 2004.

MOST CONSECUTIVE DAYS SPENT SURFING

A streak of perfect waves on 2 September, 1975, proved an irresistible invitation to a young surfer named Dale Webster, freshly relocated from San Diego to Valley Ford, California, USA. His 14-day surfing paradise extended into a 28-year mission of catching at least three waves to shore every day. Hurricane winds, sharks, car problems and kidney stones failed to interrupt Dale's daily regimen. During the years of kicking out and rolling through the mighty ocean, he married, raised a family, held several jobs, went through 30 boards and 28 wetsuits, inspired generations of riders, and developed a wastewater conservation method for the redwood groves of California. On 29 February, 2004, Dale retired the record for **MOST CONSECUTIVE DAYS SPENT SURFING** after enjoying 10 407 days among the waves.

TRIVIA

Dale's quest changed the wetsuit repair warranty to 1 year *or* 10 000 waves.

DID YOU KNOW?

The story of the 'Daily Wavester' is featured in filmmaker Dana Brown's surfing documentary, *Step Into Liquid*.

MOST ENTRANTS AT A BOG SNORKELLING WORLD CHAMPIONSHIP

Peat bogs are areas of wet, marshy ground filled with decaying plant matter. These swamps are plentiful in the UK, as is the popular sport of racing through its murky waters on foot, bike and flipper. For the past 20 years, international competitors have submerged into the Waen Rhydd peat bog located near the small town of Llanwrtyd Wells, in Wales. Wearing snorkels, flippers and wetsuits, 146 people completed 2 lengths of a 55-metre trench without using any conventional swimming strokes on 30 August, 2004. This turnout marked the **MOST ENTRANTS AT A BOG SNORKELLING WORLD CHAMPIONSHIP**. Serious bog snorkellers can now also enter the annual mountain bike and triathlon competitions.

DID YOU KNOW?

The **MOST CONSECUTIVE BOG SNORKELLING WORLD CHAMPIONSHIPS** won are three times by two competitors: Philip John (2002–2004) and Steve Griffiths (1985–1987) both of the UK.

GREATEST DEPTH BICYCLED UNDERWATER

Mountain Bike Bog Snorkelling Champions better watch out! Vittorio Innocente of Milan, Italy, combined his beloved sports of bicycling and scuba diving for a unique record-setting experience. Vittorio dived — and drove — 52.5 metres off the coast of Genoa, Italy, on 23 July, 2002, on his mountain bike, dubbed *Nautilus*. The bike was modified to stay under longer by adding lead weights, flooding the tyres, and fitting a plastic wing behind the seat. This trip registered as the **GREATEST DEPTH BICYCLED UNDERWATER . . .**

. . . Until Vittorio broke his own record on 13 July, 2005. Determined to prove that mountain bikes really could be ridden anywhere, the 59-year-old man was lowered into the ocean off Genoa again to ride through the sea mud for a total 60 metres in 45 minutes.

TRIVIA
On 4 May, 2003, Vittorio pedalled 36 minutes 38.15 seconds for another record: **FARTHEST UNDERWATER BICYCLING**. He logged 2 kilometres along the Naviglio Canal in Milan, Italy.

DID YOU KNOW?
Vittorio proves mountain bikes and riders are globally tough by cycling across Alaskan glaciers and Kenyan deserts. His odysseys help raise money for cancer research.

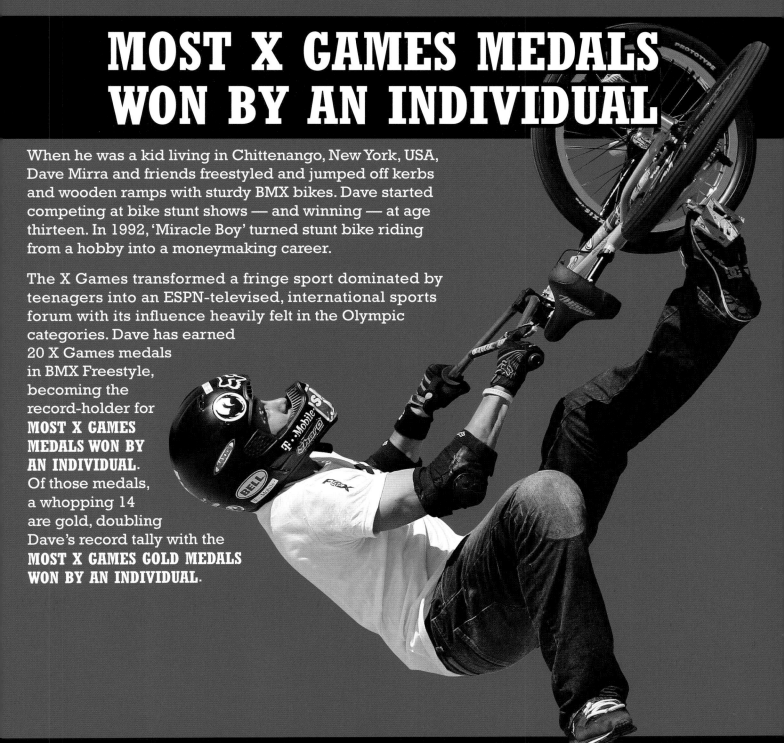

MOST X GAMES MEDALS WON BY AN INDIVIDUAL

When he was a kid living in Chittenango, New York, USA, Dave Mirra and friends freestyled and jumped off kerbs and wooden ramps with sturdy BMX bikes. Dave started competing at bike stunt shows — and winning — at age thirteen. In 1992, 'Miracle Boy' turned stunt bike riding from a hobby into a moneymaking career.

The X Games transformed a fringe sport dominated by teenagers into an ESPN-televised, international sports forum with its influence heavily felt in the Olympic categories. Dave has earned 20 X Games medals in BMX Freestyle, becoming the record-holder for **MOST X GAMES MEDALS WON BY AN INDIVIDUAL**. Of those medals, a whopping 14 are gold, doubling Dave's record tally with the **MOST X GAMES GOLD MEDALS WON BY AN INDIVIDUAL**.

TRIVIA
The 'Extreme Games' first took place in Rhode Island and Vermont, USA, during July 1995.

DID YOU KNOW?
In January 2001, Dave caught huge air and the record for **HIGHEST BMX VERTICAL AIR ON A HALFPIPE** in San Diego, California, USA. His jump off a 5.5-metre ramp achieved 5.8 metres!

DEEPEST SCUBA DIVE BY A DOG

Dwane Folsom, USA, regularly takes his dog, Shadow, scuba diving off the coast of Grand Cayman Island. The deepest the pair usually go is approximately 4 metres. When diving, Shadow wears a specially adapted diving suit made up of a helmet, weighted dog jacket and breathing tube connected to his owner's air tank. Mr Folsom rescued Shadow as a puppy from a dog pound in Boynton Beach, Florida. Shadow is a black mongrel—half retriever, half labrador.

TRIVIA

During World War II, 'para pups' were military-trained dogs able to parachute alongside soldiers and medical personnel. These canines helped carry supplies and find injured men.

MOST TENNIS BALLS HELD IN THE MOUTH BY A DOG

A golden retriever named Augie fetched prizes and a spot in the record books with his natural canine ability. The Miller family from Dallas, Texas, USA, noticed Augie loved to fetch and hold on to tennis balls when he was a mere pup. When he was age five, they entered him in Purina's Beggin'® Strips 'Stupid Dog Tricks' contest at the Grapevine Mills shopping centre in Dallas. He won the local and national competitions, leading to a meeting with Guinness World Records. Augie is the certified record-holder for **MOST TENNIS BALLS HELD IN THE MOUTH BY A DOG** after he successfully gathered and held all 5 regulation-size tennis balls — without any assistance from humans — on 6 July, 2003.

DID YOU KNOW?
The golden retriever is a dog breed naturally gifted in the ability to track and fetch objects.

TRIVIA
Augie demonstrated his talent on *The Late Show with David Letterman*.

LARGEST SIMULTANEOUS MOTORCYCLE BURNOUT

There are lots of tricks in a motorcycle rider's repertoire. A well-known trick is a 'burnout'. The motorcycle remains stationary while its rear wheel spins, creating smoke by burning the rubber on its tyre tread.

The primary rule is to prevent injuring yourself and your bike. Mass participation events rely on each rider's co-operation and plenty of organisation to get everybody doing the same thing at the same time. A total of 106 motorcycles participated in a simultaneous burnout at the Werner Rennen 2004 event at EuroSpeedway, Lausitz, Germany, on 5 September, 2004.

TRIVIA

The mecca of motorcycling is the annual Sturgis Motorcycle Rally in Sturgis, South Dakota, USA. The rally dates back to 1938. In 2005, attendance surpassed 500 000!

DID YOU KNOW?

In 1898, the Metz Company of Waltham, Massachusetts, USA, built the first US production motorcycle, the Orient-Aster. It preceded Indian (1901) and Harley-Davidson (1902) brands that are still popular today.

QUIZ ME!

Q. 1
Rob Williams sure can make a sandwich fast . . . with his feet. But who is widely credited with inventing the sandwich?

a) Monsieur Mangetout
b) John Montague, 4th Earl of Sandwich
c) Brenda Murray, 1st Empress of Eire
d) Chris Hardin, 3rd Count of Kings County

Q. 2
True or False? Toe wrestling has become so popular that it is now an Olympic event.

Q. 3
Dale Webster has been surfing every day for 28 years in California, but where did surfing originate?

Q. 4
The Bog Snorkelling World Championship is held in the British town Llanwrtyd Wells. What is Llanwrtyd Wells' other claim to fame?

Q. 5
Vittorio Innocente set a record for the **Greatest Depth Bicycled Underwater.** What do you call bicycles that can bike *on* water?

Q. 6
True or False? Dave Mirra earned 20 medals at the X Games doing bike stunts.

Q. 7
'Para pups' were used during World War II to help the military, but could these para pups win medals for their bravery?

Q. 8
The golden retriever Augie has held five tennis balls in his mouth. What else is true about golden retrievers?

a) They are famous for their outstanding scenting abilities and can be trained to carry out search and rescue work.
b) They are great family dogs because of their tolerance of children.
c) Their calm, affectionate temperaments make them wonderful guide dogs for the blind.
d) All of the above.

Q. 9
A well-known motorcycling trick is the 'burnout',but which of the following are also motorcycling tricks?

a) A 'Flamingo'
b) An 'Endo'
c) A 'Wheelie'
d) All of the above.

ANSWERS ARE ON PAGE 138

Test your *Extreme* know-how with these cool quiz questions!

EXTREME KILLER

We use our five senses of sight, sound, smell, taste and touch to avoid danger, especially from other animals. The use of *common sense* is the best defence against these **LETHAL RECORD-HOLDERS.**

MOST DANGEROUS PINNIPED

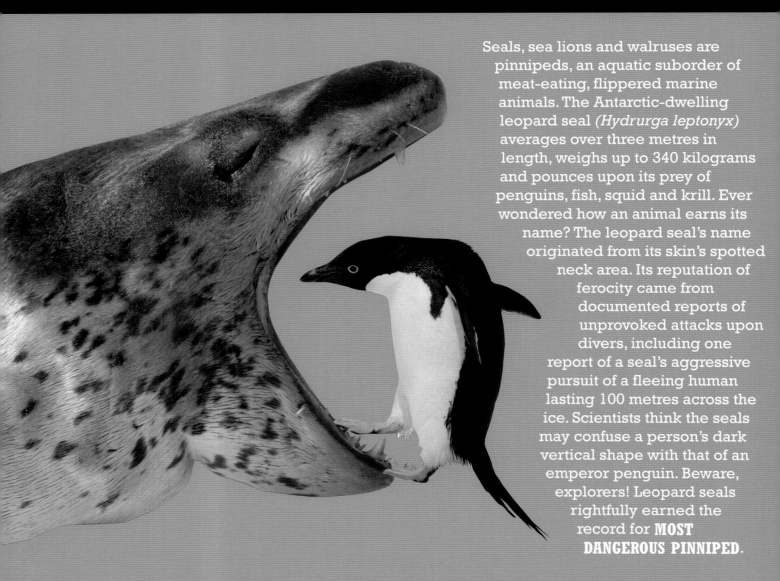

Seals, sea lions and walruses are pinnipeds, an aquatic suborder of meat-eating, flippered marine animals. The Antarctic-dwelling leopard seal *(Hydrurga leptonyx)* averages over three metres in length, weighs up to 340 kilograms and pounces upon its prey of penguins, fish, squid and krill. Ever wondered how an animal earns its name? The leopard seal's name originated from its skin's spotted neck area. Its reputation of ferocity came from documented reports of unprovoked attacks upon divers, including one report of a seal's aggressive pursuit of a fleeing human lasting 100 metres across the ice. Scientists think the seals may confuse a person's dark vertical shape with that of an emperor penguin. Beware, explorers! Leopard seals rightfully earned the record for **MOST DANGEROUS PINNIPED**.

TRIVIA
The killer whale is the sole natural predator of leopard seals.

DID YOU KNOW?
The leopard seal is the only seal species that eats other seals.

MOST VENOMOUS JELLYFISH

The sea wasp is not an insect, but it can sting you! Discovered in 1955 off the coast of Queensland, the sea wasp, known in Australia as the box jellyfish (*Chironex fleckeri*), has up to 60 tentacles. Each arm contains millions of poisonous nematocysts (small external stinging cells). One box jellyfish stores enough poison to kill 60 humans. This transparent umbrella bobs along the currents or sleeps on the ocean floor . . . until a swimmer gets too close. Chemicals on our skin activate the jellyfish's nematocysts. People have died within 4 minutes after a 'bite' by the **MOST VENOMOUS JELLYFISH**. This extreme killer is responsible for at least one death a year.

TRIVIA

You can use acetic acid, found in vinegar and human urine, to temporarily take the sting out of a jellyfish's bite before seeking immediate medical attention.

Naturalist-physician Hugo Flecker discovered a new species when local police netted the killer of several swimmers in January 1955: the box jellyfish.

DID YOU KNOW?

Some lifeguards wear Lycra stinger suits to guard their skin against the jellyfish's deadly touch.

KILLER RANKINGS

1. Blue-ringed Octopus 0.008 mg
MOST VENOMOUS MOLLUSC

2. Puffer Fish 0.008 mg
MOST POISONOUS EDIBLE FISH

3. Brazilian Huntsman Spider 0.01 mg
MOST VENOMOUS SPIDER

4. Small-scaled Snake 0.025 mg
MOST VENOMOUS LAND SNAKE

5. Poison Dart Frog 0.05 mg
MOST DANGEROUS FROG

6. Saw-scaled Viper Snake 0.151 mg
SNAKE RESPONSIBLE FOR MOST HUMAN DEATHS

7. Tunisian Fat-tailed Scorpion 0.32 mg
MOST VENOMOUS SCORPION

8. King Cobra Snake 0.35 mg
LONGEST VENOMOUS SNAKE

Watch out for these deadly record-holders! Scientists tested the natural toxins in these animals' bites, stings and skins to determine the 'lethal dose' to a mouse. (Lethal dose, or LD50, is measured in milligrams of poison necessary to kill 50% of the test subjects.)

MOST VENOMOUS LAND SNAKE

Can you guess where the **MOST VENOMOUS LAND SNAKE** lives? Australia seems to be the preferred locale for several toxic species, including the small-scaled snake (*Oxyuranus microlepidotus*). The small-scaled snake prefers slithering around the Diamantina River and Cooper Creek drainage basins in Queensland and western New South Wales. These intelligent and human-shy reptiles control the rodent population by eating rats and mice. One single strike paralyses its small prey with a mere 0.056 grams of venom. This amount is also sufficient to kill several human adults.

When 'milked', the average venom yield is 0.043 grams from an average specimen measuring 1.7 metres long. Yet one record-breaking male yielded enough potent venom to kill 15 humans or 250 000 mice with only 0.108 grams! Fortunately, no human death has been reported from this snake's bite.

TRIVIA

Milking snakes for their venom is a skill developed by snake wranglers. If done wrong, the process can be stressful for the snake and dangerous for the wrangler. Antitoxin is created from the snake's venom for treatment of snakebite victims.

DID YOU KNOW?

The branch of zoology focusing on the study of reptiles and amphibians is herpetology.

MOST DANGEROUS LIZARD

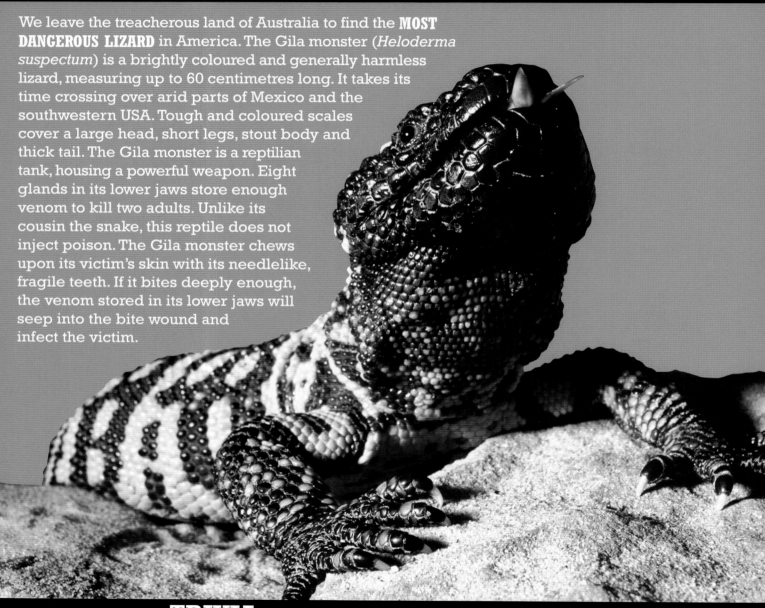

We leave the treacherous land of Australia to find the **MOST DANGEROUS LIZARD** in America. The Gila monster (*Heloderma suspectum*) is a brightly coloured and generally harmless lizard, measuring up to 60 centimetres long. It takes its time crossing over arid parts of Mexico and the southwestern USA. Tough and coloured scales cover a large head, short legs, stout body and thick tail. The Gila monster is a reptilian tank, housing a powerful weapon. Eight glands in its lower jaws store enough venom to kill two adults. Unlike its cousin the snake, this reptile does not inject poison. The Gila monster chews upon its victim's skin with its needlelike, fragile teeth. If it bites deeply enough, the venom stored in its lower jaws will seep into the bite wound and infect the victim.

TRIVIA
Beadlike scales create the Gila monster's unusual marbled skin. Its colour combinations vary between mix-and-match brown or black with orange, pink, yellow, or dull white.

DID YOU KNOW?
The name 'Gila monster' refers to the Gila River Basin in Arizona.

MOST DANGEROUS BIRD

The **MOST DANGEROUS BIRD** lives in New Guinea and north-eastern Queensland, Australia. The cassowary bird has dark feathers — except around its wattle, the brightly coloured neck area. Each foot has three forward-pointing toes with claws strong enough to grip the ground while running. This bird's not-so-secret weapon is a massive 13-centimetre-long attack spike on each foot. The cassowary is taller than the average person at almost two metres. If you're looking this bird in its penetrating eyes, then you're in trouble. The cassowary is nature's ultimate kickboxer. When threatened, the cassowary leaps into the air and kicks. The attack spike's sharpness, combined with a powerful kick, can rip open a person's stomach or cause enough blood loss to kill.

TRIVIA
There are three species of cassowary (family Casuariidae) and all of them are dangerous when wounded or cornered.

DID YOU KNOW?
Atop the cassowary's head is a bony growth called the casque.

MOST DANGEROUS ANT

The bulldog ant (*Myrmecia pyriformis*) found throughout Australia is the largest of its species at 1.75 centimetres in length. This primitive and aggressive ant is unafraid of humans. Its strong jaws and tenacious grip resemble its canine namesake. Once this ant bites down, it won't let go. But its sting is worse than its bite! The bulldog ant hangs on to a victim with its long-toothed mandibles, curls its body underneath, and thrusts its long, barbless stinger into the skin repeatedly, injecting more venom each time. Adult humans allergic to such types of venom have died within 15 minutes of an attack by the **MOST DANGEROUS ANT**.

DID YOU KNOW?

There have been at least three human fatalities attributed to bulldog ants since 1936. A farmer from Victoria, Australia, was the most recent victim in 1988.

MOST VENOMOUS SPIDER

There's not just one creepy-crawly killer to avoid, but a species of **MOST VENOMOUS SPIDER**. Its homeland is South America, but the Brazilian wandering spider (*Phoneutria*) loves to travel. Specimens have hitched rides in bunches of bananas on cargo ships sailing overseas! At 17 centimetres, this large, dark-coloured arachnid loves nesting inside clothing, blankets and shoes. If disturbed from its nap, it wakes up cranky and looking to bite the intruder. The amount of its venom injections varies, but hundreds of people report accidental bites every year.

The serious relative of this five-member species is the Brazilian huntsman spider (*Phoneutria fera*). It creates the most active neurotoxin of any living spider. Only 0.0000056 grams of the huntsman's venom is potent enough to kill a mouse.

TRIVIA

This spider is called a wandering spider because, instead of building a lair or web, it prefers to roam across the jungle floors.

QUIZ ME!

Q. 10
A leopard seal is the **Most Dangerous Pinniped**. How many documented cases have occurred of this seal species actually killing a human?

Q. 11
True or False? Jellyfish called sea wasps inject their victims with a poison that is deadlier than any snake venom.

Q. 12
The small-scaled snake is the **Most Venomous Land Snake**. Are the majority of snakes poisonous?

Q. 13
The Gila lizard is dangerous due to its venom-filled bite. How many poisonous lizards are there in the whole world?

a) 2
b) 25
c) 250
d) 2500

Q. 14
When threatened, the cassowary bird is quite dangerous. Which of the following is also true about the cassowary?

a) It is very aggressive.
b) It can fly.
c) Meat is the mainstay of its diet.
d) None of the above.

Q. 15
The **Most Dangerous Ant** is the bulldog ant species. How many species of ants are there in the whole world?

a) 10
b) 100
c) 1000
d) More than 10 000

Q. 16
True or False? The Brazilian wandering spider has been found as far away from Brazil as Britain.

ANSWERS ARE ON PAGE 138

Test your *Extreme* know-how with these cool quiz questions!

eXtreme DANGER

The nature of record-breaking is to push beyond the established limits — those set by the previous record-holder and even your own. However, nature is full of unpredictable elements that exceed our body's limitations. Extreme danger calls for extreme **CAUTION!**

MOST DANGEROUS LOVE LIFE

In the previous chapter, we learned several hazardous creatures live in Australia. This is also the homeland of the mammal with the **MOST DANGEROUS LOVE LIFE** — and the danger comes not from other predators, but from other love-struck males!

Every August is breeding season for the brown antechinus (*Antechinus stuartii*), a small marsupial mouse related to the Tasmanian devil. The entire adult male population spins out of control for two weeks in searching for not 'one true love', but as many future mates as possible. Their quest for romance is more important than eating, sleeping or surviving skirmishes against rival males. At the end of the season, almost all of the males have died from starvation, infection and ulcers caused by their stressful love life. The females, however, live on to raise the young and find love again next year.

TRIVIA
Brown antechini eat beetles, spiders, cockroaches and other bugs.

DID YOU KNOW?
In contrast to their dangerous mating battlegrounds, the nests of the brown antechini are safely located inside cosy logs and crevices.

MOST POISONOUS EDIBLE FISH

The puffer fish (*Tetraodon*) of the Red Sea and Indo-Pacific region inhales water or air and 'puffs up' to frighten predators, resembling an underwater porcupine with its scary-looking quills. The pointy skin isn't the only part of this fish that shouldn't be touched. The **MOST POISONOUS EDIBLE FISH** carries the fatal poison tetrodotoxin in its ovaries, eggs, blood, skin, liver and intestines. Ingesting less than 0.113 grams of this poison is fatal!

We know an untreated snakebite or serious burn may kill us, but a fish dinner? The delicate and dangerous Japanese dish named *fugu-sashi* (blowfish-raw) requires a highly trained and licensed chef in its preparation to ensure the diner's safe consumption. Improper slicing and dicing will cause the worst indigestion imaginable — the diner dies within 20 minutes of cleaning his plate!

TRIVIA
The **MOST VENOMOUS MOLLUSC** is the blue-ringed octopus, which also carries tetrodotoxin.

DID YOU KNOW?
Tetrodotoxin is one of the most powerful nonproteinous poisons and 1200 times deadlier than cyanide.

SHARING A BATHTUB WITH THE MOST RATTLESNAKES

Known as 'The Texas Snake Man', Jackie Bibby counts snakes among his closest friends. He should, having been trained in the professional art of snake handling since high school. Jackie has worn coiled rattlers upon his head in place of his trademark bowler; dangled 8 by their tails from his mouth (one record); crawled willingly into a sleeping bag packed with 109 not-so-sleepy reptiles (a second record); and lounged in a bathtub filled with 75 live western diamondback rattlesnakes (a third record). Bibby shared the latter record-making experience of **SHARING A BATHTUB WITH THE MOST RATTLESNAKES** with co-holder Rosie Reynolds-McCasland on 24 September, 1999. Jackie and Rosie sat in two separate, equally snake-filled bathtubs placed alongside each other on the set of *Guinness World Records: Primetime* in Los Angeles, California, USA.

TRIVIA

Interlocking rings of keratin — the same material as that in a person's fingernails — make up the noisy rattle at the end of a rattlesnake's tail.

DID YOU KNOW?

Jackie Bibby has been bitten 8 times seriously enough for hospital stays.

LONGEST DURATION OF FIRE TORCH TEETHING

Any action involving the unpredictable element of fire requires taking lots of precautions . . . and having a quick way of dousing flames at the ready. Breathing fire is extremely dangerous for the performer and audience. Improper inhalation or exhalation can cause a 'blow back', scorching the breather's lungs or burning an onlooker. This trick falls under the category of 'Do Not Try This at Home!' Serious training is required for jugglers, circus performers and magicians who learn how to manipulate special torches, fuel and breathing techniques.

Matthew J. Cassiere adopted the stage name of 'Matt the Knife' (MTK) when he became a professional performance artist, consultant, writer and multiple record-breaker in several hazardous categories. On 30 October, 2004, MTK held a lit torch vertically in his teeth for 23 seconds. This act reset the record in **LONGEST DURATION OF FIRE TORCH TEETHING**.

TRIVIA
Matt the Knife is a member of the International Brotherhood of Magicians.

DID YOU KNOW?
Matt the Knife currently holds 3 additional Guinness World Records: **FASTEST HANDCUFF ESCAPE, FASTEST UNDERWATER HANDCUFF ESCAPE** and **MOST TORCHES EXTINGUISHED IN ONE MINUTE (FIRE-EATING)**.

MOST VIRULENT VIRAL DISEASE

Ebola hemorrhagic fever causes death in up to 90 percent of its victims. While the exact origin of the disease is unknown, cases have been seen in humans since the 1970s throughout Africa. Recognition of the disease and its virulent cause occurred in 1976 when 318 people from the Democratic Republic of the Congo (formerly Zaire) became infected. Scientists hypothesise that transmission of the Ebola virus begins with an animal to a human. Patients suffer high fevers and bleeding from eyes, ears and nose. These secretions are highly contagious and the reason for the swiftness of outbreaks among family members and health-care workers. Although there is no cure yet, the disease is extremely rare, with fewer than 1200 reported deaths since its 1976 discovery. The animal source will need to be identified before transmission can be contained and a cure is developed for the **MOST VIRULENT VIRAL DISEASE.**

TRIVIA
Three of the four identified subtypes of the Ebola virus have caused disease in humans.

DEADLIEST LAKE

On the night of 21 August, 1986, a massive amount of carbon dioxide (CO_2) burst from Lake Nyos in Cameroon, West Africa. A poisonous cloud formed over the immediate area, depriving thousands of animals and 1746 people of oxygen. Survivors far enough outside of the lake's vicinity recall only falling asleep while others suffocated to death.

When scientists investigated the tragedy, they discovered several factors contributing to create the lethal combination. Lake Nyos lies in a dormant volcano crater. Perhaps the gas was volcanic in nature. Water in most lakes naturally mixes as seasons change. Tropical lakes feature steady temperatures and the water forms layers, with a lack of circulation thereby trapping any gases beneath decomposing plant materials on the lake surface. Although the gases' origins are debated, the deadly results are not. The gas lay trapped at the bottom of Lake Nyos and had enough time to turn toxic before its release on that fateful night.

Since this tragedy, scientists have been 'burping' the **DEADLIEST LAKE** — forcing out the built-up gas at regulated times and tolerable levels.

DID YOU KNOW?
An international team of scientists developed a system to 'burp' the lake by flushing the lake water through a series of pipes. These pipes forcefully circulate the water sucked from the lake bottom and jetted onto the lake surface.

QUIZ ME!

Q. 17
The brown antechinus is a mammal that is noted for having the **Most Dangerous Love Life**. What *spider* is well known for its deadly mating habits?

Q. 18
Are the Japanese aware of how dangerous it is to eat the poisonous puffer fish called *fugu-sashi*?

Q. 19
Jackie Bibby has shared quite a lot of time with rattlesnakes, but do rattlesnakes always rattle before they strike?

Q. 20
Matt the Knife is a member of what 'magical organisation'?

Q. 21
True or False? Carbon dioxide is heavier than air.

Q. 22
The Ebola virus is the most dangerous in the world. How many cases have been reported in the US?

a) 12
b) 2
c) 1
d) 0

ANSWERS ARE ON PAGE 138

Test your *Extreme* know-how with these cool quiz questions!

eXtreme SPEED

The human *NEED TO MOVE FASTER*

than our rivals began as a survival trait.

Today, we can zoom through life on foot, wing and

lawn mower, taking record-breaking to new speeds!

FARTHEST DISTANCE COVERED IN A LAWN MOWER RACE

When asked to mow the lawn, don't look at it as a boring chore . . . it's training for future glory at the lawn mower racing championships! This cutting-edge sport got its grassroots start in Britain, as a money-saving alternative to the mounting expenses of racing cars. Everyone had a lawn mower and a different style of pushing, riding or steering. The speed limit averaged, at the time, a meagre 56 kilometres per hour. (Today's riders hit 133 kph on modified machines.)

On a hazy August afternoon in 1973, the newly formed British Lawn Mower Racing Association held the first annual 12-hour world championship. Blades were removed, automatic-shutoff switches enabled, and protective gear required to pass safety inspections. Since then, the sport has sprouted into international competitions and all-ages popularity. The **FARTHEST DISTANCE COVERED IN A LAWN MOWER RACE** was 505 kilometres at Wisborough Green, UK, during the 25th annual world championship on 29–30 August, 1998. Ian Dobson, Robert Jones and Steve Williams (all UK) of the team 'Extreme Headless Chickens' mowed down the competition for the record.

TRIVIA

Edward Beard Budding invented the first hand-pushed lawn mower in 1830. He was working in a cotton mill in Stroud, England. People considered him crazy to cut grass by pushing a bladed machine, so he tested out his invention only at night.

DID YOU KNOW?

The United States Lawn Mower Racing Association organises a nationwide season, culminating in September's televised Challenge of Champions.

FASTEST FURNITURE

Couch potatoes, rejoice! You don't have to leave your comfy sofa behind to run errands, but you might have to relocate to Britain. Edd China and David Davenport (both from the UK) design and build furniture-on-the-go. Using a variety of base vehicles, these machine modifiers create speedy bathtubs, toilets, four-poster beds and a fur-covered car. The **FASTEST FURNITURE** is a motorised sofa. The fully licensed 'Casual Lofa' rumbles along UK roads at 140 kph. Its mileage reads 1000 kilometres travelled since March 1998.

The speedy sofa is powered by a Mini 1300-cc engine and steered by a medium-size pizza pan (complete with a pepperoni pizza for snacking). Two passengers can lounge while the driver uses a chocolate bar to hand-shift between the sofa's four automatic gears and a cola can for a braking system. Signal lights are housed beneath two flowerpots. The front bumper coffee table supports a clock, a TV and the speedometer.

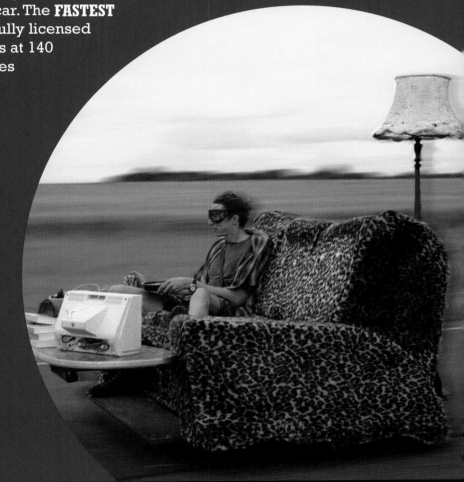

TRIVIA
The knee throttle gives the driver a choice of a feet-up or feet-down driving position.

DID YOU KNOW?
A black-and-white television provides the in-car entertainment.

AND THE WINNER IS...

12	SNAIL = 0.048 kph
11	TORTOISE = 0.27 kph
10	SLOTH [in trees] = 0.43 kph
9	HUMAN [on hands] = 2.54 kph
8	COCKROACH = 5.4 kph
7	HUMAN [running] = 37 kph
6	HARE = 48 kph
5	ANTELOPE = 56 kph
4	CHEETAH & SPUR-WINGED GOOSE [flying] = 100 kph
3	LAWN MOWER = 133 kph
2	FASTEST FURNITURE = 140 kph
1	THRUST SSC CAR = 1228 kph

FASTEST MAN AND WOMAN

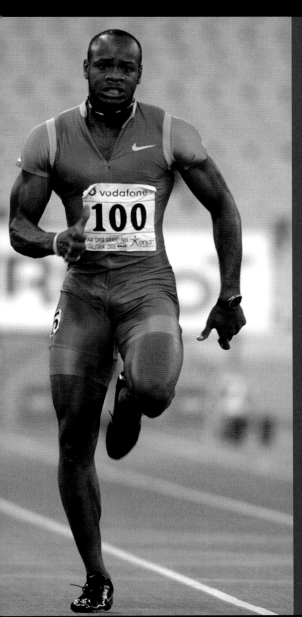

The first edition of *Guinness World Records* in 1955 recognised six co-holders for **FASTEST MAN — 100 M**. The 100-metre dash was the measuring distance for this claim and all six men had achieved 10.2 seconds as hand-timed by stopwatches, although the years and countries varied.

Times, literally, changed to electronic measurements in splitting one second into hundredths of a second. On 14 June, 2005, Asafa Powell crossed the finish line of the 100-metre dash in a blistering, record-setting 9.77 seconds. Currently, Asafa is the **FASTEST MAN — 100 M**. The companion record for **FASTEST WOMAN — 100 M** remains with Florence Griffith Joyner, who blazed through the 100-metre dash in 10.49 seconds on 16 July, 1988. Her death in 1998 at the age of 38 did not diminish her record status as, to date, her performance remains unequalled.

TRIVIA

The six original fastest men were Jesse Owens (1936, USA), Harold Davis (1941, USA), Lloyd LaBeach and Norwood 'Barney' Ewell (1948, USA), McDonald Bailey (1951, Trinidad), and Heinz Fütterer (1954, West Germany).

DID YOU KNOW?

'Flo Jo', the nickname of Florence Griffith Joyner, also set the women's 200-metre dash record at 21.34 seconds on 29 September, 1988.

FASTEST WINGBEAT OF AN INSECT

FASTEST-MOVING INSECT

People can create a sport out of *anything*. As we've seen in this chapter, all you need is a speedy object, a working stopwatch and a crowd of cheering spectators.

The legendary pastime among Russian czars was bug racing ... specifically cockroaches, a long-lived species with about 4000 different types scuttling around the world. In 1991, the University of California in Berkeley, California, USA, scientifically proved what many racing enthusiasts already knew. The **FASTEST-MOVING INSECT** record belongs to *Periplaneta americana*, a large tropical cockroach of the order Dictyoptera. The insect was clocked at 5.4 kilometres per hour. That works out to moving 50 body lengths per second!

The tiny midge of the genus *Forcipomyia* is microscopic in size, earning its nickname of 'no-see-um' ... until it bites you. As larvae, these algae-eating flies inhabit watery areas around the globe. The adults move into moist, ground-based areas, such as rotting wood, tree holes and salt marshes. Scientists tested the speed of various bugs' wingbeats and crowned the tiny midge with the title of **FASTEST WINGBEAT OF AN INSECT** for its incredible 62 760 beats per minute, achieved under natural conditions. The muscular contraction-expansion cycle of 0.00045 seconds required for such rapid wingbeats is currently the fastest muscle movement ever measured.

DID YOU KNOW?

People owe the tiny midge fly a big thankyou. This insect is the only pollinator of the cacao tree, the source of chocolate-producing cacao beans!

TRIVIA

Brisbane, Australia, is home to more than 450 cockroach species. The city hosted its 23rd annual Cockroach Races in January 2005. Over 7000 attendees participated in the charity event for a local children's hospital.

QUIZ ME!

Q. 23
True or False? The largest irrigated crop in the United States is grass.

Q. 24
Edd China and David Davenport built a speedy sofa, which travels at 140 kph. But which of the following pieces of furniture is designed to always be 'on-the-go'?

a) Cupboard
b) The Murphy Bed
c) Love seat
d) None of the above.

Q. 25
How many Olympic medals has Asafa Powell, currently the **Fastest Man – 100 M**, won?

Q. 26
We know the midge can sure 'shake a wing,' but which of the following is also true about the midge?

a) It looks like a tiny mosquito.
b) Its larvae resemble worms.
c) It can be found on every continent.
d) All of the above.

Q. 27
A cockroach is the **Fastest-Moving Insect**. Which of the following also shows the cockroach's amazing survival tactics?

a) It can live without a head for up to a week.
b) It will eat anything — including another cockroach!
c) It can live for a month without food.
d) All of the above.   *ANSWERS ARE ON PAGES 138–139*

Test your *Extreme* know-how with these cool quiz questions!

EXTREME ON THE

Determination and invention are the keys to making history. A machine is not always required to complete the journey. The real engine powering these record attempts was an individual's GET-UP-AND-GO *attitude.*

MOVE

FASTEST LAND SPEED

Land speed record attempts began in 1898 when Count Gaston de Chasseloup-Laubat of France finished a single run through a course. His average speed was 63.18 kph.

Almost 100 years later, Andy Green broke his own previous record for **FASTEST LAND SPEED** — and the sound barrier — in the seat of Thrust SSC. The supersonic car was powered by two Rolls-Royce Spey 202 jet engines, generating 50 000 pounds of thrust.

The Thrust car series consisted of three different vehicles, with the second and third cars driven to various land speed records through the years by the team of Green and Richard Noble. The first land speed record of 1020 kph, set by Richard in Thrust 2, came and went on 4 October, 1983. Andy took the third car, Thrust SSC, past Richard's mark at 1150 kph on 25 September, 1997.

Andy climbed behind the wheel again on 15 October, 1997. When Thrust SSC tore through the Black Rock Desert in Nevada at 1228 kph, or Mach 1.02, the car created a shock wave in front of it and broke through the sound barrier with a massive sonic boom.

TRIVIA
Andy Green was a Royal Air Force fighter pilot before he broke the sound barrier behind the wheel of a car.

DID YOU KNOW?
Reaching the limit in land speed and sound barrier records will depend upon the human body's ability to withstand the gravitational pressure, or G-forces, of acceleration.

The Fédération Internationale de l'Automobile (FIA) governs motor sport worldwide and officiates every land speed record attempt.

DEEPEST DIVING SUBMERSIBLE IN SERVICE

The Japanese research submarine *Shinkai 6500* is the **DEEPEST DIVING SUBMERSIBLE IN SERVICE**. The craft's name refers to its maximum depth limitation of 6500 metres. On 11 August, 1989, the vessel surpassed its own limits by 27 metres for a depth of 6531 metres in the Japan Trench off Sanriku, Japan. The 3-person craft (2 pilots and 1 researcher) is 9.5 metres long, 2.7 metres wide and 3.2 metres high. The sub is launched from a research vessel, such as *Yokosuka*. The craft is capable of submerging for up to 8 hours. Its mission is to collect samples, install observation instruments on the seafloor, and capture video and still footage underwater. The *Shinkai 6500* is a valuable tool in sea research and the continued study of geophysics, geology and earthquake prediction. Currently, it is continuing its exploration of the world's seabed.

FASTEST CROSSING OF THE ENGLISH CHANNEL BY AMPHIBIOUS VEHICLE

The journey doesn't have to stop where the road ends and the water begins . . . if you're driving an amphibious vehicle. The blending of sports car and speedboat mechanics dates back to 1899 in Denmark. Today, Gibbs Technologies of the UK offers the Aquada for road-and-water enthusiasts. The doorless hull has been tested to withstand leaks and saltwater corrosion. The vehicle reaches 161 kilometres per hour on the road and 56 kph on water. The 12-second transformation from car to boat occurs at the press of a button. Wheels retract, and the engine cues a jet to expel 1 ton of thrust, the amount of force required for a vehicle to skim across the water.

The record for the **FASTEST CROSSING OF THE ENGLISH CHANNEL BY AMPHIBIOUS VEHICLE** is 1 hour, 40 minutes and 6 seconds, achieved by Sir Richard Branson (UK), who 'drove' a Gibbs Aquada between Dover, UK and Calais, France, on 14 June, 2004.

TRIVIA

JAMSTEC's (Japan Marine Science and Technology Centre) unmanned second submersible, *Kaiko*, verified the **DEEPEST POINT IN THE OCEAN** with a test dive of 10 918 metres into the Pacific Ocean's Mariana Trench in March 1995.

FASTEST ATLANTIC CROSSING WALK ON WATER

Frenchman Rémy Bricka first crossed the Atlantic Ocean aboard a steamship. It was 1972, and Rémy decided his next crossing would be as captain of his own fate, not a passenger along for the ride.

His next crossing of the Atlantic Ocean began on 2 April, 1988. Determined to 'walk', Rémy fitted his feet inside polyester ski floats, dragged a floating pod carrying few supplies behind him, and steered with a double-headed paddle. His departure dock was Tenerife in the Spanish Canary Islands. Rémy covered 5638 kilometres, eating plankton on the way, before a Japanese trawler helped him dock in Trinidad on 31 May, 1988. Rémy's determination and extraordinary two-month journey registered as the **FASTEST ATLANTIC CROSSING WALK ON WATER.**

LONGEST DISTANCE WALKING ON HANDS

Some people like to walk the road less travelled. And then there's Johann Hurlinger, the record-holder for **LONGEST DISTANCE WALKING ON HANDS.** An Austrian man living in the early 1900s, Johann decided to give his feet a rest and let his fingers do the walking . . . or more precisely, his palms and wrists. For 10 hours each day, his hands walked from Vienna, Austria, to Paris, France. He averaged 2.54 kilometres per hour. The total distance covered in those gruelling 55 days was a muscle-aching 140 kilometres. Now there's an example of repetitive stress injury!

Johann's record has not been broken for a century. Those interested should have strong arms, tough palms, a good sense of balance, and an idea of where they're headed since they'll be keeping their eyes on the road.

TRIVIA
At home in France, Rémy Bricka plays 24 instruments strapped to his body and is called 'L'homme Orchestre', or the 'One-Man Band'.

DID YOU KNOW?
Gymnasts advise would-be record-breakers to master the handstand *first*. From there, you can take your first steps. It's just like walking . . . but upside down.

LARGEST LAND TRANSPORT VEHICLE

The 2.75-million-kilogram (2750-tonne) crawler-transporter slowly moving through Florida's Kennedy Space Centre is the **LARGEST LAND TRANSPORT VEHICLE** used for moving objects between two points. Two of these mechanical behemoths have been in operation since 1967, charged with the critical — and backbreaking — task of transporting space shuttles to and from their launch pads. Although these are *not* the **LARGEST MOBILE MACHINES**, the crawler's individual size and operating capacity are record-setting statistics. Each machine is 6 metres high, 40 metres wide, 35 metres long, and runs on 8 giant tank-style tracks. The family car may get a flat tyre, but these crawlers need a new 908-kilogram 'shoe' if a track becomes worn.

A mission starts when the crawler picks up its load from the vehicle assembly building. This is a fully assembled space shuttle, mounted on a mobile launcher platform, and weighing another 454 tonnes! A loaded crawler averages a speed of 1.6 kilometres per hour on its way to the launching pad.

TRIVIA
The crawlers run on the Crawlerway, a 40-metre roadway as wide as an 8-lane freeway and viewable from space.

DID YOU KNOW?
A laser docking system guides the crawler into position for loading.

BIGGEST SKATEBOARD

Foundation Skateboards founder and skater Tod Swank believes life should be lived to the extreme — in a radical, alternative, uniquely sized, revolutionary manner. So why not grab a bunch of fellow skating pals to build the **BIGGEST SKATEBOARD**? Construction on the WBS (World's Biggest Skateboard) started in 1996 in San Diego, California. Certification by Guinness World Records was achieved on 4 October, 2004. Tod shares design and production credit with Greg Winter, Dana Hard and Damon Mills. The giant board stretches 3.6 metres long. Riders can stand on the 1.2-metre-wide surface, after they boost themselves 75 centimetres off the ground to get aboard. Its hot rod wheels were donated by a sports car. Its scaled-up double trucks turn when the board is tilted, just like on a regular-size skateboard. Five riders on board, working together, can surf the sidewalk without falling off. The only problem — no brakes on 230 kilograms of runaway board!

TRIVIA
The design team's next dream: a truly gigantic skateboard about the size of a car, but this time with a fully operational braking system!

DID YOU KNOW?
The WBS is rolling through promotional stops across America, but watch out: other skaters are trying to build an even *bigger* board!

QUIZ ME!

Q. 28
When Andy Green broke the sound barrier with his Thrust SSC, it caused a sonic boom. Can a sonic boom hurt you?

Q. 29
The *Aquada* offers a speedy way to get across the English Channel, reaching speeds of 56 kph on water. What's a more common (not to mention faster) way to cross the English Channel?

Q. 30
The *Shinkai 6500* is capable of surveying approximately what percentage of the world's oceans?

a) 12 percent
b) 98 percent
c) 66 percent
d) None of the above.

Q. 31
What insect can walk on water, and without the polyester ski floats that keep Rémy Bricka afloat?

Q. 32
What do Adho Mukha Vrksasana and a normal handstand have to do with each other?

Q. 33
Since the two NASA crawler-transporters have been in use, how many kilometres, in total, have they travelled?

Q. 34
True or False? The first skateboard was developed in the twentieth century by surfers who made them using rollerskates.

ANSWERS ARE ON PAGE 139

Test your *Extreme* know-how with these cool quiz questions!

EXTREME SOUNDS

In our modern age, we race through life with a right earpiece for our phone and a left earpiece for our digitised playlists. We ask others if they can hear us **OVER THE NOISE** *— while our musical world plays on around us.*

DEEPEST NOTE IN THE UNIVERSE

The **DEEPEST NOTE IN THE UNIVERSE** is a B-flat, 57 octaves below middle C. It's the song of a dying galaxy and has been playing for about 2.5 billion years!

A supermassive black hole in the centre of the Perseus cluster of galaxies — 250 million light-years away — generates acoustic waves through a thin layer of surrounding gases. We can't hear it, because the decibel level (dBA) is more than a million billion times lower than the human ear can detect. Professor Andrew Fabian of Cambridge University led astronomers in this discovery after 270 hours of observations at the Chandra X-ray Observatory.

TRIVIA

NGC 1275, aka Perseus A, is the giant galaxy at the centre of the cluster.

DID YOU KNOW?

The collapse of a massive object, such as a star, forms a region of space-time known as a black hole. Nothing, not even light, escapes its gravitational pull.

LOUDEST BURP

Some maestros try to make music out of the noises made by the human body during the act of digestion. For a burp, your stomach releases gases that rise up through your oaesophagus and out of your mouth. Different cultures either declare this rude behaviour or applaud its proper commentary on a good meal. Fizzy beverages, such as carbonated sodas, and gassy foods, such as cauliflower or broccoli, can cause big-time burps.

Paul Hunn of the United Kingdom released the **LOUDEST BURP** in the London offices of Guinness World Records on 20 July, 2004. Officials measured the burp's sound from 2.5 metres away, and 1 metre high from Paul. His burp measured a whopping 104.9 decibels on a certified and calibrated class 1 precision measuring noise-level meter. Paul's bellyful was an earful: his decibel level was higher than a pile driver heard from a distance of 30.5 metres!

LOUDEST SNORE

Snoring is a sign of respiratory problems, an annoyance and noisy sleep disturbance, but not technically a 'talent' according to Guinness World Records. However, they did recognise the extraordinary sound level of the **LOUDEST SNORE** by Kåre Walkert of Sweden. On 24 May, 1993, Kåre's recorded peak snoring levels tipped the noise level meter at 93 dBA. The snore's decibel equivalent is a jackhammer breaking up concrete heard from 15 metres away! The loud outbursts are symptoms of the breathing disorder apnoea from which Kåre suffers. Relaxed throat muscles, enlarged tonsils or adenoids, or a long uvula block the airway. Breathing becomes laboured and louder, until the sleeper falls silent . . . unable to breathe. The brain releases adrenaline to awaken the sleeper and restore proper circulation of oxygen, blood and carbon dioxide. Snorers, and their suffering companions, should seek out the advice of their physician. Sometimes the solution is as simple as changing sleeping positions for a real good night's sleep.

DID YOU KNOW?
Paul Hunn's secret combination for boisterous burps: fizzy soda and big gulps of air!

TRIVIA
Sleep apnoea is very common, afflicting an estimated 5 percent of Australians.

DID YOU HEAR THAT?

LOUDNESS and decibel level depend on how near your ear gets to the source of the sound. Noises below 30 dBA are often ignored, with **PAIN** experienced around 130 dBA. Noises over 160 dBA instantly perforate the eardrum and cause permanent deafness.

1. Lab-created **HORN** blown = **210 dBA**
   (*sound bored holes through solid material*)

2. **BLUE WHALE** = **188 dBA**

3. Woman's **SCREAM** = **129 dBA**

4. **WHISTLING** = **125 dBA**

5. Military **JET AIRCRAFT** taking off = **120 dBA**

6. Front row at a **ROCK CONCERT** = **110 dBA**

7. **SNAPPING** fingers = **108 dBA**
   (*and lawn mower heard from a metre away*)

8. African **CICADA** = **106.8 dBA**

9. **BURPING** = **104.9 dBA**

10. **SNORING** = **93 dBA**
    (*and jackhammer heard from 15 metres away*)

11. **CAR** going 105 kph, heard from 7.5 metres away = **80 dBA**

12. **CLAPPING** hands = **73 dBA**

13. **CONVERSATIONAL SPEECH** from 30 centimetres away = **60 dBA**

14. **BIRD CALL** = **40 dBA**

LARGEST ANIMAL ORCHESTRA WITH THE MOST MEMBERS

In 2000, Americans Richard Lair and David Soldier composed a melodious method of promoting the conservation of the endangered Asiatic elephant. The humans founded the 12-piece Thai Elephant Orchestra, also known as the **LARGEST ANIMAL ORCHESTRA WITH THE MOST MEMBERS**. The musicians' ages range between 7 and 18 years old. These music-loving pachyderms perform improvised and traditional melodies using a variety of specially designed percussion and wind instruments. Humans cue them at the piece's opening and closing, but the elephants select the notes and rhythms. David accompanies the 'ellies' as lead violinist in traditional Thai tunes, plus a sampling of classics from Beethoven to Hank Williams. All types of audiences are invited to attend their concerts held at the Thai Elephant Conservation Centre in Lampang, Thailand. The band doesn't tour, but their second album, *Elephant Rhapsodies*, is on sale, with a third in the works.

TRIVIA
David Soldier has coached songbirds in the use of brass instruments.

DID YOU KNOW?
Elephants paint! Keep a look out for another pachyderm pastime later on in this book.

LARGEST SIMULTANEOUS YODEL

People think yodelling is a wildly pitched song warbled only between Alpine mountain people, yet many cultures — European, African, Hawaiian, Mexican and American — use this songlike cry in communication and entertainment.

There are solo-yodelling records for longest and loudest, with the category of **LARGEST SIMULTANEOUS YODEL** bringing in the crowds. On 5 October, 2002, a group of 937 yodellers sang the popular Swiss tune, *Von Luzern uf Wäggis zue*, for more than one minute. The event took place at the Ravensburger Spieleland in Meckenbeuren, Germany.

The current record holder is Yahoo! Inc., the global Internet company based in Sunnyvale, California. The company known for its yodelling corporate theme gathered 1795 people at its headquarters on 19 November, 2004. Wylie Gustafson, the original Yahoo! yodeller, alongside the winner of the company's yodel challenge, 9-year-old Taylor Marie Ware, showed the others the proper way to yodel their way through a record attempt.

TRIVIA
The American style of yodelling is influenced by European and African styles. Popular singers, such as Gene Autry and Hank Williams, rapidly shifted vocal tones between normal and falsetto in their songs.

MOST DJS IN RELAY

DJs were in heavy demand and rotation at London's Bridge and Tunnel Club during a charity event and record attempt. An Internet-based music club, d-train, celebrated its first anniversary by setting the record for **MOST DJS IN RELAY**. Starting at 7:00 pm on 18 June, 2003, 'disc jockeys' jumped behind the decks to spin one record each, with every mix continuous, synchronous, and to professional standards for 4 hours. At least one person had to be moving and grooving on the dance floor throughout the show. A total of 59 DJs shared their eclectic range with a mash-up of beats from Afro, hip-hop, house and drum 'n' bass. At the dropping of tune No. 51, this harmonious event broke the previous Guinness World Record spun by 50 musical hosts.

DID YOU KNOW?
DJs select and play sound recordings, but they can also manipulate the output and create original compositions through various techniques of cueing, sampling, cutting, scratching and beat-matching.

QUIZ ME!

Q. 35
True or False? A black hole is a hole.

Q. 36
True or False? Britiain's Paul Hunn sure can burp, but is it true that in some cultures burping is okay, and even polite?

Q. 37
Sleep apnoea, or snoring, is quite common. Which of the following are other sleeping disorders?

a) Somnambulism
b) Narcolepsy
c) Bruxism
d) All of the above.

Q. 38
The Elephant Orchestra is quite talented, but what do 'Little Elephant Saddle', 'Floating down the Pin River', 'Pin Pia', 'Bamboolin', 'Dancing with Prathida', and 'Kaw-Liga' have to do with them?

Q. 39
The term 'DJ' refers to 'disc jockey'. What is a modern play on this term?

Q. 40
While yodelling can be found in many cultures, where did it start?

ANSWERS ARE ON PAGE 139

Test your *Extreme* know-how with these cool quiz questions!

EXTREME SMELLS

In our world today, a great deal of time, money and effort is put into smelling the 'right' way. These record-breaking

TOUGH ODOURS & MIGHTY SNIFFERS

overwhelm the senses to leave a lasting impression.

MOST SENSITIVE NOSE FOR A LAND MAMMAL

Nature equipped the **LARGEST LAND CARNIVORE** with powerful hunting tools for survival amid the Arctic's harsh living conditions. Temperatures below -50° F don't slow down a polar bear insulated with two layers of fur and a 12-centimetre-thick layer of blubber. The hunter's tools consist of impressive size (up to 3 metres tall), bulky weight (up to 600 kilograms), sharp claws for fishing, a stomach capacity of 68 kilograms, ice-proof footpads, and the **MOST SENSITIVE NOSE FOR A LAND MAMMAL**. This fierce hunter follows the faintest whiff of a possible future meal — even if its prey is 30 kilometres away and under thick ice. Bears have been documented walking in a straight line for 32 kilometres, running hundreds of kilometres from shore across ice, and swimming 100 kilometres in pursuit of a fleeing seal.

The polar bear also hunts walruses (500 kilograms) and the world's **LARGEST PREY**, beluga whales (600 kilograms). It should also be noted that the polar bear's digestive system, being more suited to processing meat rather than vegetation, makes it the most carnivorous of its species.

TRIVIA

Cubs born in early wintertime stay in the snow den until early springtime. They are born blind, toothless and completely dependent upon their mother for warmth and food.

DID YOU KNOW?

The scientific name for the polar bear is *Ursus maritimus* or 'sea bear'.

MOST ACUTE SENSE OF SMELL

Insects don't have noses like other animals, but they do have sensitive antennae and use these feelers to guide them in search of food, safety and love! The male emperor moth (*Eudia pavonia*) rules over the insect kingdom with its impressive skill in locating its mate. This orange-hued flier, found throughout Europe and Asia, boldly flits about in daylight. Its mate, although larger in size by about 7 centimetres, is a soft grey colour and moves cautiously during night-time. According to the results of German experiments carried out in 1961, the **MOST ACUTE SENSE OF SMELL** in the insect world belongs to the male emperor moth. Its antennae chemoreceptors can detect a female moth from 11 kilometres away with only one molecule of her pheromones.

TRIVIA
Metamorphosis from caterpillar to moth does not include the formation of mouthparts. Adult emperor moths live for only a few weeks, long enough for mating season, then die afterward from starvation.

DID YOU KNOW?
The four 'eyespots' on the emperor moth's wings are used to confuse and frighten predators.

MOST FEET AND ARMPITS SNIFFED

The average human being can recognise approximately 10 000 different smells. Laboratories, such as Hill Top Research in Cincinnati, Ohio, USA, hire olfactory testers, or professional sniffers, in the development and testing of health and personal care products. After 15 years of being an olfactory tester, Madeline Albrecht and her discerning nose broke into the record books with **MOST FEET AND ARMPITS SNIFFED**. Madeline had personally verified the effects of the lab's odour-reducing products upon approximately 5600 feet and thousands of armpits by the year 2000. Now that's a professional hard at work!

TRIVIA

Anosmia is the medical term for being unable to detect or recognise any odour.

DID YOU KNOW?

The feet have 250 000 sweat glands and excrete about half a pint of moisture every day!

SMELLIEST FLOWER

The *Amorphophallus titanum* is an impressive sight since it blooms once every 1 to 3 years, usually in the Sumatran rainforests in Indonesia, and lives for a brief span of a few days. Spiked, burgundy-coloured petals unfurl and the tuber shoots skyward, achieving the stately heights of 2 metres to 3.35 metres. Since 1889, horticulturists have been able to cultivate this flower under controlled conditions in parts of Europe and the United States. Within a city's botanical exhibit, curious onlookers lean in for a whiff of the rare tropical flower blooming. And then everyone, except scavenger animals and flies, beats a hasty retreat for the door.

The odour released by the **SMELLIEST FLOWER** resembles decaying meat, and you can catch the scent of the 'corpse flower' a kilometre away! The bloom's odour and the petals' meaty colour attract carrion bugs to help with pollination. Two to four days from the flower's blooming, the plant itself dies.

TRIVIA
In 1878, Italian botanist Dr Oroardo Beccari discovered the corpse flower among the rainforests of Indonesia.

DID YOU KNOW?
The corpse flower also has the **LARGEST BLOOM**. On 23 May, 2003, the Bonn University's Botanical Gardens cultivated a 3-metre-high sample of this dual record-holder in Bonn, Germany.

LARGEST GARLIC FESTIVAL

Rivalries among record claims exist even at a city level. In 1978, Dr Rudy Melone, president of Gavilan College in Gilroy, California, USA, read a news article about a tiny French village claiming to be the garlic capital of the world. He decided the world needed to taste the truth: the garlic soup in Arleux, France, might be tasty, but it wouldn't hold a candle to the fire-breathing, homegrown creation cooked up by Gilroy's chefs!

Since 1979, the last weekend in July has attracted garlic lovers numbering in the millions for the three-day, aromatic Gilroy Garlic Festival. The **LARGEST GARLIC FESTIVAL** honours this vegetable's place in the world and attracts 130 000 people each year! Garlic farming is the major business of Gilroy, and all proceeds from the festival are fed back into the community. Every festival kicks off with the lighting of a 7.6-metre fake bulb of garlic. Participants then sample a wide range of garlic-flavoured food — everything from meat to ice-cream — whipped up by enthusiastic volunteers!

TRIVIA

The ancient Egyptians and Greek Olympians held garlic, also known as the 'stinking rose', in high esteem.

DID YOU KNOW?

Cooking up chemistry in your kitchen! When you chop up a garlic clove, the mixing of acid cells and fibre create allicin. This chemical blocks certain infectious organisms — and also gives garlic its powerful smell!

QUIZ ME!

Q. 41
Polar bears are huge carnivores. These hunters have sharp claws, a stomach capacity of 68 kilograms, and the **Most Sensitive Nose for a Land Mammal** — but can they outrun a human on land?

Q. 42
The male emperor moth can detect a female moth from 11 kilometres away with the scent of only one molecule of her pheromones. What exactly is a pheromone?

Q. 43
'Anosmia' is the medical term for being unable to detect or recognise any odour, but what's the medical term for being able to smell?

Q. 44
True or False? The *Amorphophallus titanum*, or 'corpse flower', can be as tall as a grown man.

Q. 45
We know that garlic is used in many recipes, even ice-cream, and is good for you, but when did people first start eating it?

ANSWERS ARE ON PAGE 139

Test your *Extreme* know-how with these cool quiz questions!

eXTREME
EXTEN

Some people are born into record-making history while others make their mark with their own sense of style. You'll have to extend your ruler **A FEW MORE CENTIMETRES** for these lengthy record-breakers!

SIONS

SMALLEST WAIST ON A LIVING PERSON

Cathie Jung, USA, born in 1937, who stands at 1.72 m, has a corseted waist measuring 38.1 cm. Un-corseted, it measures 53.34 cm. Her enthusiasm for Victorian clothes is why at the age of 38 she started wearing a 15.24 cm training belt to gradually reduce her then 66.4 cm waist. She has never had surgery to define her waist. Since 1983, she has worn a corset 23 hours a day, only removing it for her daily shower. The mother of three, who does not eat a special diet or exercise to maintain her waist, says: 'We had no intention of setting a record. It was about dressing appropriately for the age'.

LONGEST NOSE ON A LIVING PERSON

In 1897, Edmond Rostand wrote a famous dramatic stage play, *Cyrano de Bergerac*, about a sensitive man challenged in life by the considerable length of his nose. In 2001, a different man, named Mehmet Ozyurek, enjoys the fuss other people make over his impressive nose.

Turkish-born Mehmet is a construction worker in his hometown of Artvin. The Black Sea region of the country is known for celebrating the size of its people's noses. There is an annual long-nose competition where both men and women line up against a ruler made of anchovy bone. Mehmet stuck out against 22 other nasally inclined rivals to be declared the proud winner. Guinness World Records used a more standard ruler to verify the measurements on 31 January, 2001. Mehmet's nose, extending 8.78 centimetres from the bridge to the tip, was declared the **LONGEST NOSE ON A LIVING PERSON.**

TRIVIA
Historical accounts from the 1770s state that a circus performer named Thomas Wedders had a nose measuring 19 centimetres—the **LONGEST NOSE EVER**!

DID YOU KNOW?
Cyrano de Bergerac was a real-life French soldier and writer in the 17th century.

THEY GO TO GREAT LENGTHS!

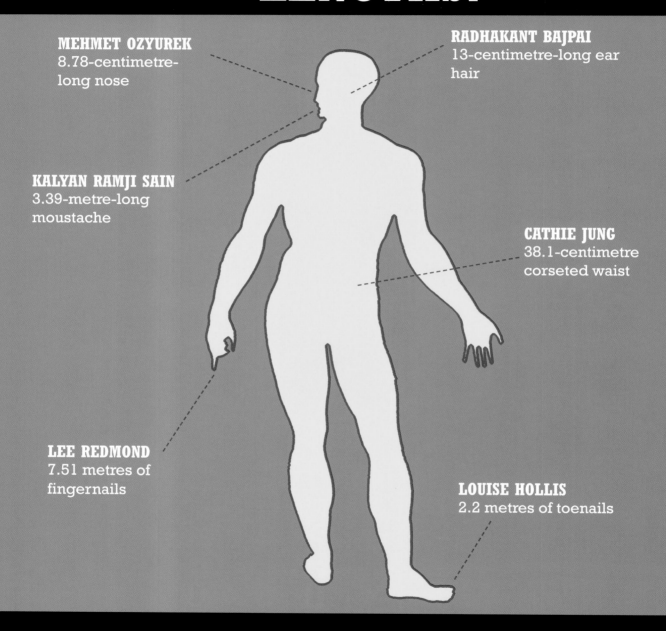

MEHMET OZYUREK
8.78-centimetre-long nose

RADHAKANT BAJPAI
13-centimetre-long ear hair

KALYAN RAMJI SAIN
3.39-metre-long moustache

CATHIE JUNG
38.1-centimetre corseted waist

LEE REDMOND
7.51 metres of fingernails

LOUISE HOLLIS
2.2 metres of toenails

LONGEST EAR HAIR

Growing the **LONGEST EAR HAIR** doesn't affect your hearing for better or worse, but it does earn a spot in the record books. Radhakant Bajpai is a 50-year-old grocer and dedicated family man living in Naya Ganj, Uttar Pradesh, India. A previous record-holder, fellow Indian B. D. Tyagi of Bhopal, inspired Radhakant to reconsider his own ear's naturally hairy extensions. As of May 2003, the strands sprouting from the middle of the pinna, or centre of Radhakant's outer ears, stretched to an impressive 13 centimetres at their longest point! Dr R. P. Gupta confirmed the measurements uprooted the previous record, and Radhakant became an official entrant into the archives. 'Making it into *Guinness World Records* is indeed a special occasion for me and my family,' he said.

TRIVIA
Our hair and earwax trap dirt and germs to protect the inner ear from infection.

DID YOU KNOW?
Although we hang earrings and rest eyeglasses upon the pinna (or auricle), its true purpose is to funnel sound into the ear canal.

HEAVIEST WEIGHT LIFTED WITH A HUMAN BEARD

Give Lithuanian Antanas Kontrimas's beard a tug and you'll be swept off your feet! This record-holder for whiskery feats of strength has strapped several items to the ends of his chin hairs and swung them clear off the ground, including a keg of his homemade beer, a sack of grain, a local TV host, and then the **HEAVIEST WEIGHT LIFTED WITH A HUMAN BEARD**. Antanas lifted a girl weighing 63.1 kilograms, 10 centimetres off the ground on the set of *El Show De Los Records* in Madrid, Spain on 25 May, 2006.

TRIVIA
The beard of Antanas Kontrimas has also towed a Land Rover, a sports plane and a jeep with 5 passengers. He's training to lift a man and to haul in a fishing trawler.

DID YOU KNOW?
Antanas Kontrimas has not shaved for more than 25 years and his 50-centimetre beard is the longest in his hometown of Telshiai, Lithuania.

LONGEST MOUSTACHE

Moustache care is more involved than beard growing, because the owner must clip and sometimes wax the moustache ends, also known as the tips . . . while a beard owner can just sit back and let nature take its course. Measuring a full beard is fairly straightforward for officials, and everybody else — done lengthwise, the ruler starts at the chin and finishes at the tip of the beard's longest whisker. Certifying the length of a moustache is a bit more divided, literally, by the nose. Measurements are still in length, but the ruler is used width-wise to determine the moustache's combined size in amount of hair grown on the right and left sides of the face.

Ram Singh Chauhan of India believes that someday he will be in the record books with his moustache. Yet he falls short of the record at the current length of only 1.97 metres. The **LONGEST MOUSTACHE** belongs to Kalyan Ramji Sain of India, who started his facial hair care in 1976. By measuring time in July 1993, his moustache had reached a record-setting span of 3.39 metres. Although he is attentive to his hair's needs, the right side measured 1.7 metres, while the left side was only 1.67 metres.

TRIVIA
The previous moustachioed record-holder in India was Karna Ram Bheel, serving a life sentence in a New Delhi jail. In 1979, he tended all 2.38 metres of his moustache with mustard, oil, butter and cream.

DID YOU KNOW?
Genetics, diet, stress and proper care affect all types of hair follicles responsible for healthy hair growth.

LONGEST COMBINED FINGERNAIL LENGTH

The nails covering our fingers and toes often give doctors a peek into our stomachs. How is that possible? Nails are a form of modified hair, with the plates of a nail made up of a protein called keratin. The nail bed is the connective tissue beneath the plate. Any serious illness will cause a groove in the nails known as Beau's lines. These grooves make the patient's medical history visible to the eye of a practised doctor, nutritionist or manicurist.

American Lee Redmond knows the secret of good nail care: you are what you eat. Lee eats plenty of protein and soaks her incredible fingernails in warm olive oil. She never chews on them — that would be a considerable meal because Lee has been letting her fingernails grow since 1979. She wanted to see how long she could grow her nails before they twisted . . . except they didn't, so she kept growing them, and growing, and growing . . . ! Her **LONGEST COMBINED FINGERNAIL LENGTH** is 7.51 metres — prompting people to ask Lee, 'Who does your nails?'

TRIVIA
Shridhar Chillal of India is the man with the **LONGEST FINGERNAILS ON A SINGLE HAND**. His left hand's little finger has a nail measuring 1.38 metres!

DID YOU KNOW?
Fingernails grow on average 0.5 millimetres per week — four times faster than their foot counterparts!

LONGEST TOENAILS

Another American woman decided she wanted pretty feet to show off in her fashionable summertime sandals, so she started growing out her toenails. In 1991, the **LONGEST TOENAILS** were a combined length of 2.2 metres — so each nail is approximately 22 centimetres long . . . and a different shade of toenail polish. Louise Hollis just couldn't bear to file those lovely nails down once the summer had ended. Her 12 children and 21 grandchildren lend a hand to help Louise paint and file her unique 'collection'. Louise enjoys the attention her colourful nails cause when she's out and about in her hometown of Compton, California.

TRIVIA
Louise Hollis sassily chose her nails over a frustrated spouse when he gave her the ultimatum, 'It's me or the nails!' Her reply, 'I've had you for 21 years, but the nails are new.'

DID YOU KNOW?
Nails and hair do not grow after death. The skin dehydrates, giving the appearance of longer nails and hair.

GREATEST EAR SLINGSHOT

Monte Pierce of Bowling Green, Kentucky, USA, holds an 'ear-ie' talent. The human ear's auricle (or pinna) has no bone; its lower fatty part is the earlobe. Monte has been tugging on his earlobes all his life. The **LONGEST STRETCHED EARLOBES** can touch tips beneath Monte's chin, yet doctors determined Monte's hearing was unaffected by his stretching. He can stretch his right earlobe to 11.4 centimetres and his left to a full 12.7 centimetres!

Then Monte discovered his adjusted lobes had an extreme talent for lobbing. Monte builds up the skin's elastic energy by tugging on his earlobes. Then he places a coin on his ear and — just like a slingshot — lets go of the stretched lobe. The skin's built-up kinetic energy lobs the coin across the room. On 29 October, 1999, Monte stretched his earlobe to nearly 12 centimetres and set a coin flying off it for a total distance of 3.31 metres. This record for **GREATEST EAR SLINGSHOT** was set in the Los Angeles, California, studio of the *Guinness World Records: Primetime* TV show.

TRIVIA

The Suya tribespeople in Africa wear discs of wood in their ears to elongate them.

DID YOU KNOW?

The skin's elasticity allows the earlobes to snap back into place after being stretched — if done for brief amounts of time.

QUIZ ME!

Q. 46
If polydactylism occurs in as many as 2 in every 1000 births, who are some famous polydactyls?

Q. 47
Edmond Rostand's *Cyrano de Bergerac* is a famous play about a sensitive guy with a huge nose. Has it ever been made into a movie?

Q. 48
Radhakant Bajpai grew the **Longest Ear Hair**, but does everyone have ear hair?

Q. 49
Antanas Kontrimas has a record-breaking beard. Which of the following fictional characters also have famous beards?

a) Gandalf from J.R.R. Tolkien's *The Lord of the Rings*
b) Papa Smurf (from the *Smurfs*)
c) Dumbledore from *Harry Potter*
d) All of the above.

Q. 50
We know that the hair that grows on the top of your lip is known as a 'moustache', but what is a 'moustachio'?

a) A type of Turkish car
b) A flavour of ice-cream
c) A term for a large moustache
d) None of the above.

ANSWERS ARE ON PAGE 139

Q. 51
What is the name for those white spots that you sometimes see under your fingernails?

Q. 52
Louise Hollis certainly knows how to pamper her toenails, but is painting your toenails or getting a pedicure a modern phenomenon?

Q. 53
Are there cultures where stretched earlobes, like Monte Pierce's, are desired?

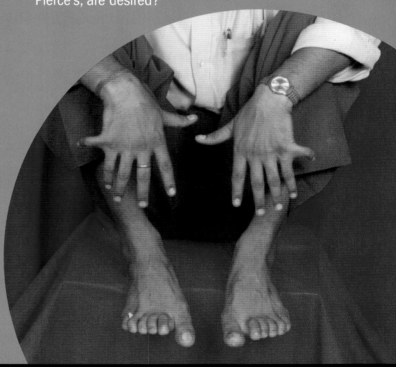

Test your *Extreme* know-how with these cool quiz questions!

EXTREME TEETH

Teeth are primarily for chewing and, in extreme cases **ATTACK AND DEFENCE.**

In this category of toothy competitors, the bravest dentist would have nightmares after seeing how these record-breakers strain the limits of dental care.

STRONGEST BITE

Do you know where the strongest muscle in your body is located? In your mouth! The masseter muscle controls the jaw's movements in talking, chewing and biting. The 'bite force' is the amount of pressure applied by the masseter upon an object. Scientists measure these levels using a bite-meter (or gnathodynamometer).

The Lerner Marine Laboratory in the Bahamas recorded the **STRONGEST BITE** using a bite-meter designed just for sharks. Marine biologists tested tiger, lemon and dusky sharks by stuffing the meter inside a mackerel. At 2 metres long, the dusky shark (*Carcharhinus obscurus*) registered a force of 132 pounds of pressure between its jaws. At the tip of its teeth, that equals 22 *tons* of pressure. That's the same as being crushed by 10 cars!

Curious about the bite force of the **LARGEST PREDATORY FISH**? So are biologists because, in theory, a bigger animal should exert a higher bite force . . . but no-one has yet recorded any official measurements between the jaws of the biggest fish, the great white shark. Meanwhile, paleontologists are learning more about evolution through the reconstruction and bite-force tests of fossilised dinosaur jaws.

TRIVIA

Marine biologist James Snodgrass designed the bite-meter for sharks: the Snodgrass gnathodynamometer. (Try saying that fast 10 times!)

DID YOU KNOW?

The great white shark can grow to more than 4.5 metres. It has several rows of teeth, with approximately 3000 sharp replacements for the teeth lost every week.

TOOTHSOME TRIVIA

While the Largest and Strongest teeth have their place, what about the average? The average adult human has thirty-two teeth (if they brush!) But among the animal kingdom, we are just one of many species.

- Turtles and tortoises are toothless. Instead of teeth, they use their horn-covered jaws to tear food into small enough pieces to swallow.

- Giraffes, like humans, have 32 teeth. Giraffes' teeth have deep grooves for stripping foliage from twigs.

- Crocodiles and alligators have 60 to 80 teeth respectively, but can grow up to 2000-3000 teeth during their lifetime. When a crocodile or alligator wears down their teeth, they can shed and regrow them. Over a lifetime, a crocodile can produce 40 sets of teeth!

- Giant armadillos' 100 teeth are largely wasted. These insect and plant eaters consume food whole, using their long mucus-covered tongues to digest food.

- Dolphins can average having 200 small, sharply pointed teeth, ideal for grasping slippery fish and squid.

HEAVIEST VEHICLE PULLED WITH TEETH

Humans grow two sets of teeth in a lifetime. The first set of 20 'milk' teeth arrive during the teething stage of 6 months old. The second set — growing beneath the first — pushes out the old ones, tooth by tooth, between the ages of 6 to 12 years old. Since the adult set of 32 teeth is your *final* natural set, your dentist isn't kidding about the importance of taking good care of your teeth.

Dentists might not approve of these record-holders' toothy hobby of weight lifting. On 31 March, 1990, Walter Arfeuille earned his record for **GREATEST WEIGHT LIFTED BY TEETH** in Paris, France. Walter held a total weight of 282 kilograms off the ground by a distance of 17 centimetres. On 18 October, 2003, Velu Rathakrishnan broke Walter's previous record of **HEAVIEST VEHICLE PULLED WITH TEETH** at Kuala Lumpur Railway Station, Malaysia. Velu pulled two KTM commuter trains, weighing an astonishing total of 293 tonnes, for a distance of 4.2 metres!

HEAVIEST SHIP PULLED BY TEETH

Archeologists have dug up the truth about dentists: ancient civilisations knew about and practised dental surgery. This included the forceful removal of diseased teeth with primitive tools. Somehow this knowledge, dating back to the Indus Valley civilisation of 3300 BCE, was lost during the confusion of the Middle Ages. This was a time when people would visit a 'barber surgeon' to have hair cut, beards shaved *and* teeth pulled. Another alternative was a 'tooth drawer', a performance artist who yanked a patient's teeth for others' entertainment. Today, people visit licensed dentists for the proper care and removal of problematic teeth.

Omar Hanapiev from Russia hopes to never lose a tooth by any of these methods since he depends on each and every one — plus several muscles — during his record attempts. Just like Velu and trains, Omar specialises in being a tooth-tower of vehicles. On 9 November, 2001, he set the record for **HEAVIEST SHIP PULLED BY TEETH**. Omar towed the tanker *Gunib* a distance of 15 metres in the port of Makhachkala, Russia. A rope tied his teeth to a ship weighing 576 tonnes. People cheered that day because he didn't lose a single tooth.

TRIVIA
The Chinese invented the bristle toothbrush in 1498. The bristles were hog hairs tied to handles made of bone or bamboo.

DID YOU KNOW?
Seventeenth-century barbers also began the cosmetic practice of teeth whitening. Teeth would be filed down to strip away the stained enamel and then 'brightened' with nitric acid.

LARGEST MAMMAL JAW

A multiple record-holder for its astonishing size, the sperm whale (*Physeter macrocephalus*) on average grows to between 12 to 20 metres long. A male specimen, tipping the scales at nearly 25 metres, yielded a lower jaw of 5 metres in length! The **LARGEST MAMMAL JAW** was exhibited in London's Natural History Museum. As you would guess, sperm whales are also the **LARGEST-TOOTHED WHALES**. Although the teeth in the upper jaw never erupt through the gums, the lower jaw contains about 50 to 60 conical-shaped teeth. Each tooth is approximately 18 centimetres long and weighs a kilogram! When the whale shuts its mouth, its massive lower teeth fit snugly into sockets located in the upper jaw.

The sperm whale swims in the open oceans, except for the chilly polar seas, and is capable of diving to the greatest depths on a hunt for giant squid, another oversize record-holder. In 1991, a sperm whale dived to a depth of 2000 metres in the Caribbean Sea. The **DEEPEST RECORD DIVE BY A MAMMAL** lasted for 1 hour 13 minutes. The **LARGEST ANIMAL BRAIN**, at 9 kilograms, also fits inside this whale's truly big head.

TRIVIA
The title character of Herman Melville's classic naval tale, *Moby Dick*, is a sperm whale.

DID YOU KNOW?
Think the sperm whale is the biggest fish in the sea? Wrong times two! Whales are mammals that breathe air and are not classified as fish. The **LARGEST MAMMAL** is the blue whale, bigger than any dinosaur skeleton. One male blue whale measured 27.5 metres in length and weighed 187 tonnes.

LAND MAMMAL WITH THE MOST TEETH

Mammals are a classification of warm-blooded animals having backbones, hair-covered skin and the ability to bear their children alive instead of laying eggs. Thankfully, the **LAND MAMMAL WITH THE MOST TEETH** isn't interested in taking a bite out of us. The giant armadillo (*Priodontes maximus*) uses its approximately 100 teeth lining the inside of its long snout for pest population maintenance. It is nature's biggest exterminator of termites and ants, yet today it is also one of the most endangered animals. It has been overhunted for its meat and killed by farmers mistaking it as a crop eater. Found in South America, the giant armadillo burrows through soil in search of bugs and a nesting place.

These amazing creatures are recognised by a distinctive armoured shell, but the giant armadillo is too large at 90 centimetres to curl its massive underbelly beneath its armour. Instead, it owns the **LARGEST CLAWS** of the animal kingdom. Its front, central claws measure 20 centimetres long. The armadillo uses both teeth and claws to rip apart the termite mounds towering throughout the region or to dig a fast getaway tunnel.

FASTEST TIME TO HUSK A COCONUT USING ONLY TEETH

Rajesh Prabhu, a 26-year-old man of Bahrain, was having a bad day until he saw a monkey trying to open a coconut. Rajesh wondered if any human had tried to husk a coconut in the same efficient manner: using hands, feet and teeth. Then Rajesh learned about Sidaraju S. Raju, the record-holder for **FASTEST TIME TO HUSK A COCONUT USING ONLY TEETH**.

Sidaraju comes from a family of farmers in Magadi, India. His love of trying new things led to applying his teeth in a unique manner. On 30 March, 2003, Sidaraju sunk his teeth into the brown fibre containing the fruit of the coconut palm tree. The coconut measured 78 centimetres and weighed 4.8 kilograms. Within 28.06 seconds, the husk was gone and Sidaraju had entered the record books.

TRIVIA
Certain species of armadillo spend 80 percent of their lives either dozing or asleep.

DID YOU KNOW?
Copra is the edible white meat inside of the coconut and is used to make coconut oil.

QUIZ ME!

Q. 54
True or False? The masseter muscle is the strongest muscle in your body.

Q. 55
Record holders for tooth-tugging vehicles need strong teeth. Not brushing or flossing can lead to which of the following dental problems?

a) Halitosis
b) Gingivitis
c) Periodontitis
d) All of the above.

Q. 56
True or False? People used to believe that pulling out bad teeth would cure other illnesses.

Q. 57
The sperm whale has the largest jaw, teeth and brain, and is capable of diving deeper than other animals in search of food. Do all of these record-breaking features guarantee a long life?

Q. 58
The giant armadillo is the **Land Mammal with the Most Teeth**. Are its teeth very sharp?

Q. 59
When Rajesh Prabhu saw a monkey husk a coconut, it inspired him to try the same with his teeth. Can monkeys be trained to harvest coconuts?

ANSWERS ARE ON PAGE 140

Test your *Extreme* know-how with these cool quiz questions!

eXtreme FOOD

Multiple competitive events focusing on food – the art of its preparation, the speed in its cooking, and the amount one human can consume – have sprouted in popularity around the globe. Our focus is on several record-breaking **CULINARY MASTERPIECES** *that tip the weight scales before anyone takes a single bite!*

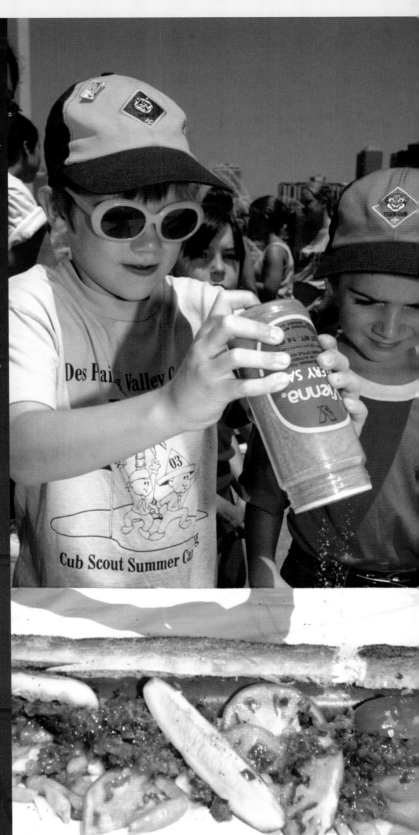

LARGEST BUBBLEGUM BUBBLE BLOWN

Chad Fell, USA, blew a bubblegum bubble with a diameter of 50.8 cm without using his hands at the Double Springs High School, Winston County, Alabama, USA, on 24 April, 2004. The secret of his success, says Chad, is blowing with three pieces of gum!

DID YOU KNOW?

The first patent for bubblegum was issued in 1869 to William F Semple, a dentist from Ohio, USA.

LARGEST ICE-CREAM SUNDAE

Having trouble deciding which flavour to choose for your sundae at the local ice-cream parlour? Imagine scooping enough ice-cream to create a sundae weighing 25 tonnes! That's what it would take to break the current record held by the Edmonton, Canada-based Palm Dairies for sculpting the **LARGEST ICE-CREAM SUNDAE**. On 24 July, 1988, this gigantic confection officially weighed 25 000 kilograms!

Controversy swirls around several claims of inventing the first ice-cream sundae. The definition of a sundae is a serving of ice-cream with a topping (syrup, fruit, nuts or whipped cream). The choice and amount of its sweet ingredients depend on a person's likes and dislikes. Purists claim it all comes down to a scoop of vanilla beneath chocolate syrup. The whipped cream and cherry on top are extraneous. US president Thomas Jefferson reportedly favoured maple syrup on his vanilla ice-cream, yet no-one called his after-dinner snack a 'sundae'.

Chilled treats made from the milk of horses, buffalo, yaks, camels, cows and goats have been traced to China's T'ang Dynasty (618–907 AD). Americans discovered the popular frozen dessert sometime in the 1770s. Today, the USA makes more than 1.5 billion gallons of ice-cream a year.

LARGEST COLLECTION OF POTATO CHIP BAGS

People love to collect things because the item — a postcard, matchbook or ticket stub — reminds them of their pleasant experience at that vacation spot, restaurant or event. These souvenirs range from childhood toys to expensive antiques, from zany buttons to colourful traffic cones. Collections are as unique as collectors, who consider the search for, and finding of, new items a serious personal quest.

Bernd Sikora of Germany started his collection in 1993, and the record really is 'in the bag'. Today, he owns 1482 potato chip bags from 43 countries. This is the **LARGEST COLLECTION OF POTATO CHIP BAGS** known to exist. The saying is true — Bernd could not stop after 'just one'.

RECIPE FOR A RECORD-BREAKER

- 20 tonnes of ice-cream (any flavour)
- 4.5 tonnes of syrup
- 240 kilograms of toppings
- Plenty of spoons

DID YOU KNOW?

Potato chips were stored in tins or barrels before the invention of the airtight, sealed bag.

LARGEST GINGERBREAD MAN

Gingerbread can be rolled and patted and shaped into edible figures of people, animals and houses. These ginger-flavoured cookies, bread and cakes have a baking history dating back to the eleventh century in Western Europe. Such treats were made and sold at local fairs, with many customs and fanciful tales passed down about the eating of gingerbread.

The **LARGEST GINGERBREAD MAN** did not come from Germany, a country rich in traditions, fairytales and recipes for gingerbread. Instead, Canada unveiled this gigantic cookie on 19 November, 2003. Chefs working at the Hyatt Regency Hotel in Vancouver baked and presented a gingerbread man measuring 4.25 metres tall, 1.72 metres wide, and 5 centimetres deep. He weighed 170 kilograms!

A baker and his team from Rochester, Minnesota, USA, are hoping to catch this record with their attempt at the 2006 Baker's Convention. John Fish of the Gingerbread House Bakery hopes the 4.55-metre gingerbread man stays intact, since no parts are allowed to break off and run away before the measurements are complete.

RECIPE FOR A RECORD-BREAKER
· 100 kilograms of flour   · 20 kilograms of shortening
· 20 kilograms of white sugar
· 20 kilograms of molasses (refined sugar syrup)
· 4 kilograms of ground ginger   · 3 kilograms of baking soda
· 3 kilograms of sea salt   · 3 kilograms of ground nutmeg

TRIVIA
The German word for gingerbread is *lebkuchen*.

DID YOU KNOW?
Ginger comes from the underground root of the ginger plant, grown throughout Asia, Japan, the West Indies, South America and western Africa.

LARGEST BOX OF POPCORN

The largest box of popcorn was made by CINEBOX with a volume of 48 m³ having been filled in 8 hours at an event in Salt Gerona, Spain on 15 September, 2005.

CINEBOX CINEBOX CINEBOX

Ven el
15 de
septiembre
desde las
12:00 am.

DID YOU KNOW?
Pieces of 4000-year-old popcorn were found in the 'Bat Cave' of New Mexico.

LARGEST ANNUAL FOOD FIGHT

Food fights are messy fun when you're in the middle of one, but everyone dreads the clean-up. Consider living in the town of Buñol, Spain. Since 1944, a week-long celebration there at the end of August has paid tribute to the town's patron saint, Saint Louis, with parties, fireworks and parades. The good time culminates in *La Tomatina*, the **LARGEST ANNUAL FOOD FIGHT**. The end of the tomato-growing season yields tonnes of surplus tomatoes perfect for squishing and throwing among excited citizens and tourists. Tomato juice stains the crowds and runs 30 centimetres deep through the crowded streets. In 2002, the fruity festival hit a milestone — *splat!* — when 38 000 people threw a total sum of 125 000 kilograms of tomatoes.

TRIVIA

How did this wild food fight start? The clouded origins include mischievous boys and spilled fruit carts. Tomatoes ended up being thrown and the annual tradition stuck.

DID YOU KNOW?

After *La Tomatina* is over, fire engines unroll powerful hoses and spray down the tomato-soaked streets and people.

QUIZ ME!

Q. 60
True or False? If you swallow bubblegum, it will stay in your stomach for years.

Q. 61
Although the origins of the ice-cream sundae are obscure and disputed, what US city claims to be the 'Home of the Ice-Cream Sundae'?

Q. 62
Bernd Sikora certainly likes his potato chips. What US state should he thank for their potatoes?

Q. 63
True or False? Ginger can calm an upset stomach.

Q. 64
Giant statues of Godzilla and King Kong have been sculpted out of popcorn. Has there ever been a movie made where these two fictional monsters actually fight each other?

Q. 65
Food fights are often thought of as taking place in school cafeterias, but in what country's legislature did a food fight erupt in 2004?

a) Zimbabwe
b) The United States
c) Taiwan
d) Greenland

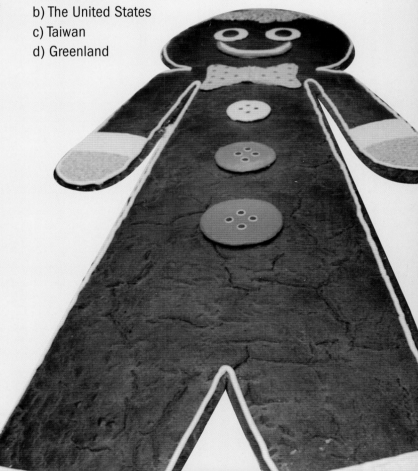

ANSWERS ARE ON PAGE 140

Test your *Extreme* know-how with these cool quiz questions!

eXtreme LUXUR

No matter how much people complain about the cost of living, there will always be those **BIG SPENDERS** willing to pay extravagant amounts for the shiniest, priciest and oddest objects just because they MUST own them! The price tags of these pursuits break records and bank accounts!

IES

DINING OUT AT THE HIGHEST ALTITUDE

True friendship is priceless and doesn't have limits . . . but sometimes safety harnesses are in order. A group of experienced mountain climbers took formal dining to new heights on 3 May, 2004. Seven out of a ten-member expedition dressed for **DINING OUT AT THE HIGHEST ALTITUDE** by wearing tuxedos as they trudged out from base camp. Their destination: a friend's 30th birthday dinner with a killer view from the top of Lhakpa Ri, Tibet.

The mountaineers, including a professional butler, scaled the summit carrying tables, chairs, silver cutlery, flowers, candelabras and a five-course meal. Hurricane winds at the peak relocated their dining site a few metres lower on the mountain — at an astonishing 6800 metres! Henry Shelford was the guest of honour. Joshua Heming served caviar, smoked duck, chocolate bombe, cheese, wine and birthday cake to the extreme diners: Thomas Shelford, Nakul Misra Pathak, Robert Aitken, Robert Sully (all UK), and Caio Buzzolini (Australia). Everyone ate and made merry, until they realised the climb back down was still ahead.

TRIVIA

A survivor of a lung tissue disease, Henry Shelford organised the climbing dinner to raise money for the British Lung Foundation.

DID YOU KNOW?

Lhakpa Ri is located across the glacier from the formidable climber's peak of Mount Everest.

MOST EXPENSIVE CAR REGISTRATION

Folklores in different cultures claim good luck will be yours upon finding certain objects, such as a heads-side-up penny or a four-leaf clover — or performing specific activities, such as tossing spilled salt over a shoulder or knocking on wood. Many cultures believe that certain numbers are lucky (7) or unlucky (13).

Buying an object to guarantee your good fortune might cost you a fortune! On 19 March, 1994, a government auction in Hong Kong, China, sold the **MOST EXPENSIVE CAR REGISTRATION** to an eager buyer for a staggering amount of money. Albert Yeung Sau-shing paid $13 million for one car licence plate. The plate simply stated '9' and nothing else. The word 'nine' is identical to 'dog' in Cantonese pronunciation, and according to cultural logic, this specific licence plate was extremely lucky to own in 1994, the Year of the Dog.

TRIVIA
The Chinese zodiac has 12 animal signs and each animal is repeated every 12 years. The Year of the Dog repeated in 2006, with its next return scheduled for 2018.

DID YOU KNOW?
The printing of licence plates for any type of vehicle, and the associated rules of registration, are different in every part of the world.

MOST VALUABLE COMIC

Comic books developed from cartoons printed in newspapers during the late nineteenth century. A series of 'comic strips' were collected and printed in a magazine form that was called a 'comic book'. This new art form became incredibly popular during World War II because the format weighed less than hardback books, had lots of colourful pictures, was easy to read, and cost only a few cents.

Today's best-known comic book publishers are DC Comics and Marvel Comics. Their band of recognisable superheroes — Batman, Superman, X-Men, and the Fantastic Four — have soared in popularity, with these adventures now appearing in comic books, novels, animated TV shows and movies.

The **MOST VALUABLE COMIC** is the 1939 first edition of Marvel Comics. Jay Parrino's The Mint, a company dealing in rare coins, comics and photographs based in Kansas City, Missouri, USA, paid $350 000 for 'Pay Copy' *Marvel Comics No. 1* in November 2001. This edition was called the 'Pay Copy' because its cover and seven pages listed the artist and pay scale. For example, artist Frank R. Paul received only $25 for his now-legendary cover.

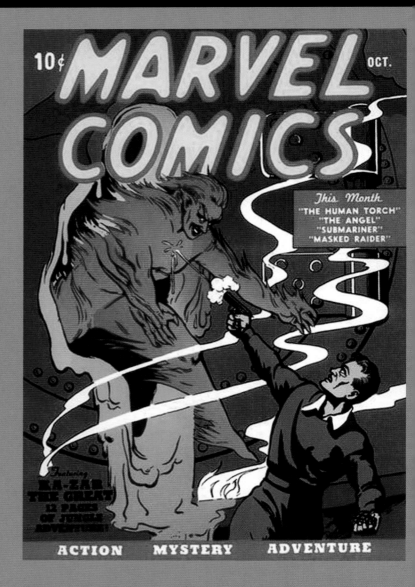

TRIVIA

Marvel Comics was originally called Timely Comics. DC Comics was originally an abbreviation of *Detective Comics*, the flagship title for National Periodical Publications.

DID YOU KNOW?

The golden age in American comic book history (1938 to the early 1950s) introduced a new art form that blended colourful images and short stories about fictional superheroes.

MOST VALUABLE BASEBALL CARD

WAGNER, PITTSBURG

In 1903, a historic series of baseball games was played between the Pittsburgh Pirates and the Boston Americans. At the time, this unnamed competition consisted of nine games, with the championship team determined by the most games won. The Boston team won the fifth game and the championship with Game 8. This challenge would become the famous World Series. The Pirate shortstop during the inaugural game was Honus Wagner, who would become a member of the Baseball Hall of Fame and the sought-after face on the **MOST VALUABLE BASEBALL CARD**.

In 1909, the Pirates were playing against the Detroit Tigers for the World Series title. Candy and tobacco companies promoted this beloved sport inside their packages by giving away cardboard cards printed with the players' names and faces. Card number 486 in a 514-card set known as the T206 series featured Honus Wagner — and he was not happy about it. Honus reportedly was upset that his face was being used to promote the sale of tobacco to kids. His card became a rare find among collectors. So rare, in fact, that even in the 1930s, his 50-cent card sold for 50 dollars. On 15 July, 2000, one of these rare cards surfaced during an online eBay auction. American Brian Seigal paid the price of $1 265 000 for this elusive piece of baseball history.

TRIVIA
An uncut printer's sheet featuring Honus Wagner's card was supposedly found folded up in an old baseball uniform also belonging to Wagner.

DID YOU KNOW?
The online marketplace, eBay, was founded in September 1995.

MOST VALUABLE DINOSAUR BONES

Owning a piece of history is a costly, and valuable, investment — especially if the purchase is made for the benefit of future generations. On 12 August, 1990, explorers from South Dakota's Black Hills Institute for Geological Research were exploring the foothills when they stumbled across a gigantic discovery: the **LARGEST AND MOST COMPLETE TYRANNOSAURUS REX SKELETON**. The skeleton was 90 percent complete and measured 4 metres tall and 12.5 metres long.

Nicknamed 'Sue', the dinosaur's bones sparked a debate of ownership among the land's owners, the town, the researchers and the American government. Finally, after numerous legal battles, a judge determined Sue's skeleton and any monies from its sale belonged to the private rancher who owned the land. Sue was sold at the famous auction house of Sotheby's in New York on 4 October, 1997. A group of sponsors donated funds to help The Field Museum of Chicago, Illinois, afford the $8 362 500 price tag. But the sticker shock was worth it, because the **MOST VALUABLE DINOSAUR BONES** have fascinated millions, young and old, since going on display at museums across America.

TRIVIA

'Sue' is named after explorer Sue Hendrickson, who first noticed the buried dinosaur bones.

DID YOU KNOW?

Tyrannosaurus rex is Latin for 'tyrant lizard king'. Field Museum staffers spent approximately 3500 hours on cleaning and repairing just the skull!

MOST EXPENSIVE CHOCOLATE BAR

THIS BAR OF CHOCOLATE WAS TAKEN FROM THE BOAT "DISCOVERY" ON ITS RETURN FROM CAPT. SCOTT'S EXPEDITION TO ATTEMPT TO REACH THE SOUTH POLE IN 1905

A bar of chocolate can be purchased at many convenient places, such as vending machines, for a handful of coins. British explorer Captain Robert Falcon Scott desperately needed any type of food, especially that quick rush of sugar and caffeine provided by chocolate, during his second fateful trip to the South Pole. This doomed expedition wiped out all of Scott's supplies, and he and his entire crew perished in 1912.

However, on his first exploration of Antarctica from 1901 to 1904, Scott and his men had plenty of chocolate. They towed 1600 kilograms of cocoa and chocolate on their frigid trek. Many bars survived, including a piece only 10 centimetres long. This prized bite of history fetched $687 at a special Polar Expeditions auction held by Christie's of London. An anonymous buyer bought the **MOST EXPENSIVE CHOCOLATE BAR** on 25 September, 2001.

TRIVIA
Captain Robert Scott died during his unsuccessful race to the South Pole against rival explorer Norwegian Roald Amundsen.

DID YOU KNOW?
Sir Ernest Shackleton, also a famous Antarctic explorer, journeyed with Scott during part of the 1901-1904 expedition.

MOST EXPENSIVE ELEPHANT PAINTING

Do you remember the orchestral members of gigantic proportions? Those talented musicians performed at the Thai Elephant Conservation Centre in Lampang, Thailand. The centre also runs an elephant hospital and training school. Thai elephants in captivity were mainly used in moving huge trees for the logging industry. But in 1989, when the government changed its laws regarding this business, unemployed *mahouts* and their elephants went to the school for help in learning a new career. Some elephants picked up a musical instrument. Other elephants picked up a paintbrush.

A group of these talented painters created a masterpiece titled *Cold Wind, Swirling Mist, Charming Lanna I*. The viewing and sale of this unusual painting was held on 19 February, 2005, at the Maesa Elephant Camp in Chiang Mai, Thailand. The **MOST EXPENSIVE ELEPHANT PAINTING** sold for $39 000 to Phanit Warin, formerly of Chiang Mai, now living in northern California. All monies are donated to the care and conservation of Thailand's elephants.

TRIVIA
In 1997, Russian-born artists Vitaly Komar and Alex Melamid journeyed to Thailand and became art teachers for the elephants.

DID YOU KNOW?
An elephant trainer is a *mahout*.

MOST EXPENSIVE COMMERCIALLY AVAILABLE DOMESTIC ROBOT

The way of the future is a world filled with mechanical helpers. Robots range in size and function between miniscule search engines in our computers to average-size humanoids designed not only to look 'more human' in appearance but to mimic our actions. These extreme machines can talk, walk, run, lift, dance and survive in the harshest environmental climates — from volcanic pits to the vacuum of outer space. The latest models resemble our household pets, free of allergy-causing hair and with a bark-mute mode. Will these metallic wonders provide the same comfort level as our families and furry friends?

Thames, a Japanese manufacturer, broke through into the household market with their TMSUK IV robot. This 'woman in a dress'-shaped robot specialises in household care and personal assistance. It first rolled across the public stage on 23 January, 2000, during a robotics show held in Tokyo, Japan. The 100-kilogram robot stands 1.2 metres tall, with an original price tag of $43 037. Today, inflation has raised the price tag to $49 508! The **MOST EXPENSIVE COMMERCIALLY AVAILABLE DOMESTIC ROBOT** runs errands, never complains, is trained in giving massages to humans, and can be operated by remote control.

TRIVIA

The city of Fukuoka, Japan, has been declared a robot test zone. Developers can operate inventions in public areas, providing they have an up-to-date licence.

DID YOU KNOW?

In 1495, Leonardo da Vinci drew plans for the construction of a mechanical man.

MOST EXPENSIVE TRIP TO SPACE BY A TOURIST

A little more than a century ago, the idea of people paying to fly on gigantic planes across the country was believed to be an impossible dream. Today, the skies are filled with passenger-crowded jets operated by many different airlines. Cars, boats and trains are everyday modes of transportation. But what about trips around the moon?

American businessman Dennis Tito wanted a phenomenal vacation and paid the steep price of $20 million to Russia for a visit to the International Space Station (ISS). A former NASA engineer, Dennis blasted off on 28 April, 2001. He spent six days floating around the station, snapping photos of Earth, peering out the portholes, and listening to opera. He splashed down on 6 May, 2001, with plenty of souvenirs of the **MOST EXPENSIVE TRIP TO SPACE BY A TOURIST**.

The following year, South African Internet millionaire Mark Shuttleworth also paid Russia the same price for the same amount of time spent visiting the ISS. He took off on 25 April, 2002, and landed on 5 May, 2002. Is this the first step toward a family vacation on Mars?

TRIVIA
Space Adventures, the Arlington, Virginia-based travel agency, arranged the details of both out-of-this-world vacations.

DID YOU KNOW?
Wall-mounted sleeping bags on the ISS prevent sleepers from walking or floating away in the gravity-free environment.

QUIZ ME!

Q. 66
Henry Shelford and his friends ate opposite the famous Mount Everest. Why is Mount Everest such a formidable challenge to climbers?

Q. 67
The number 13 is often considered unlucky, but do people actually fear it?

Q. 68
A series of comic strips printed as a collection is called a comic book. But what's another name for a longer, more complex, comic book?

Q. 69
What are the only two companies that currently produce major league baseball cards?

Q. 70
'Sue' is the current record-holder for **Most Valuable Dinosaur Bones**. What does the name *Tyrannosaurus Rex* literally mean?

a) Thunder Lizard
b) Tyrant Lizard King
c) Deceptive Lizard
d) None of the above.

Q. 71
Everybody loves chocolate, right? However, what country consumes more chocolate per capita than any other nation?

a) Switzerland
b) The United States of America
c) Belgium
d) Mexico

Q. 72
The elephants of the Thai Elephant Conservation Centre are not only talented musicians, but also talented (not to mention expensive!) painters. Where can you see a selection of elephant art?

Q. 73
TMSUK IV is the **Most Expensive Commercially Available Domestic Robot**. You may have heard of the AIBO®, a robot that is designed to look and act like a dog. Which of the following can the AIBO® do?

a) Recognise more than 100 words
b) House sit by using video and photo recording
c) Lick your face when you wake up in the morning
d) Both 'a' and 'b'.

Q. 74
True or False? Since Mark Shuttleworth's trip to space, the International Space Station has stopped having tourists come to space.

ANSWERS ARE ON PAGES 140–141

Test your *Extreme* know-how with these cool quiz questions!

eXtreme
APPET

The table manners and diets of these record-holders would turn heads in any restaurant, especially when one of them **DEVOURS THE SILVERWARE** instead of the food on his plate!

ITES

MOST WORMS EATEN IN 30 SECONDS

How much could you eat in 30 seconds? Proper dining etiquette — and your frowning parent — forbids the gobbling of a meal. But every second counts in record-breaking. The type of food in the bowl will greatly affect your attempt's success or failure. Which kind of meal do you think would be easier to swallow: solid, round candies eaten with a chopstick or hundreds of wiggly, slimy earthworms with no silverware allowed?

If your name was C. Manoharan, better known by his friends as 'Snake' Manu, then option No. 2 is your best bet. A twenty-something man from Tandaiarpet, India, 'Snake' Manu got his nickname after years of fascination with reptiles. After a while, he taste-tested one and it became his favourite meal. 'Snake' Manu had no problem with a bowl full of 200 live earthworms. He simply tipped the bowl up to his lips and — *gulp!* — swallowed its entire contents and the record for **MOST WORMS EATEN IN 30 SECONDS**. Each freshly picked earthworm measured at least 10 centimetres long and was fully consumed within the time limit. 'Snake' Manu enjoyed his homegrown meal in Chennai City, India, on 15 November, 2003.

TRIVIA
'Snake' Manu can 'snake floss' using the connective space behind his nose and mouth. He feeds small snakes into his mouth and the reptiles slither out his nose.

DID YOU KNOW?
An earthworm eats its own weight in food every day.

FASTEST ENTRAPMENT BY A PLANT

The land-based Venus flytrap and its underwater cousin, the bladderwort plant, invite plenty of bugs to dinner — as the main course. These carnivores catch lots of flies and microscopic aquatic creatures. The bladderwort plant catches its meals on the water's current, but the Venus flytrap creates a honey-type substance called nectar. The sticky and sweet liquid tempts a hungry bug right inside the plant's mouth.

The 'mouth' of both plants is really a two-hinged leaf with teeth. The upper surface of the leaf is lined with sensitive hair cells that are triggered by a bug's movements. When an insect triggers two of these cells in a row, the leaf snaps shut and the 'trap' is sprung. The plant secretes special enzymes to digest the insect, providing the plant with the nitrogen it needs to grow. The Venus flytrap 'swallows' its prey in one-tenth of a second while the bladderwort plant closes its hidden trapdoor in just $\frac{1}{15\,000}$th of a second. These two will never share a meal, but they do share the record for **FASTEST ENTRAPMENT BY A PLANT**, split between land- and water-based diners.

TRIVIA

The bladderwort plant (*Utricularia vulgaris*) is rootless and floats upon the surface of ponds, marshes and tropical waters.

DID YOU KNOW?

The Venus flytrap (*Dionaea muscipula*) grows on the coastal plains of North and South Carolina.

WHAT'S ON THE MENU?

Take your stomach on a tour around the world. Here's a sample of other people's favourite dishes!

APPETISERS

★ In Japan, tomato sauce is poured over rice.

★ An expensive Russian delicacy, caviar, comes from fish eggs.

★ Locust swarms feed a lot of people. Cambodians pop a peanut inside the bug and pan-fry it.

★ Salted licorice is a popular candy in Holland and Sweden.

MAIN COURSE

★ Seaweed is dried and eaten in the Philippines and Japan.

★ In Thailand, giant water bugs are served with chilli and sticky rice. Dung beetles add spice to curry dishes.

★ Black pudding, a breakfast dish in the UK, is made by cooking pig's blood until it solidifies.

★ Sheep heads are skinned, broiled and eaten in parts of the Mediterranean.

★ In Barbados, flying fish is a breaded, pan-fried dish *and* a symbol in the country's crest.

★ People cook and eat armadillo meat in areas of Central and South America.

STRANGEST DIET

Diet fads come and go every week. The sensible diet is a healthy one approved by your personal doctor that combines the right amount of daily exercise with balanced meals of proteins, vegetables, fruits, starches, calories and vitamins. So you probably shouldn't partake in the **STRANGEST DIET** from Monsieur Mangetout.

Michel Lotito of Grenoble, France, is better known as Monsieur Mangetout, the man who can safely eat and completely digest metal and glass. Since 1959, Mangetout has been consuming a daily average of almost a kilogram of metal. By October 1997, estimates placed the total amount of metal consumed by him at a whopping 9 tonnes! Although doctors have analysed his digestion and learned his gastric juices have a metal-corrosive foam, they still are unable to explain how this man's body has digested the following metallic morsels: 18 bicycles, 15 shopping carts, 7 TV sets, 6 chandeliers, 2 beds, a pair of skis, a computer and a Cessna light aircraft. He also managed to devour an empty coffin.

TRIVIA
Bananas and hard-boiled eggs give Monsieur Mangetout indigestion.

DID YOU KNOW?
Mangetout is French for 'eat everything'!

MOST HAMBURGERS STUFFED IN THE MOUTH

The hamburger is a popular meal around the world. But just holding a burger in your mouth *without* biting down, chewing or swallowing? You might choke — remember, record-breaking can be dangerous!

The **MOST HAMBURGERS STUFFED IN THE MOUTH** requires more than three regulation-size burgers (including buns and condiments) to be held in the mouth at the same time and the participant is not allowed to swallow any part of the hamburgers. That dog named Augie would gladly give up his tennis balls to hold one hamburger in his mouth, but this is a human-only competition. American Johnny Reitz first performed his cheek-stretching feat on the set of the TV show *Guinness World Records: Primetime*, in Los Angeles, California, on 17 June, 1998. He set the record at three hamburgers.

FASTEST TOMATO SAUCE DRINKER

American Dustin Phillips set the record for **FASTEST TOMATO SAUCE DRINKER** back in 1999. Although many have tried, no-one has yet out-slurped him.

Dustin liked sauce, lots of it, on his food. One night at dinner, friends dared him to drink the rest of the tomato sauce bottle. That was back in college, and his first attempt resulted in quite a mess. But then he began practising, whetting the taste buds daily with a full bottle, until his skills were unmatched.

On 23 September, 1999, Dustin went to Los Angeles, California, intent on sharing his talent with the world. Dustin took the stage on the set of the TV show *Guinness World Records: Primetime*. The drinking straw was 50 millimetres in diameter. The bottle was one standard 400-gram tomato sauce bottle. Dustin slurped 91 percent of the bottle's contents through his straw within 33 seconds.

TRIVIA
At the 2004 Singaporean World Record Contest, competitors also tried — and failed — to break the fastest-drinking-tomato sauce-through-a-straw record set in 1999 by Dustin Phillips.

DID YOU KNOW?
The citizens of Hamburg, Germany, enjoyed a ground beef patty sandwich called a 'Hamburg steak' in the late nineteenth century.

LARGEST BARBECUE

Eating is a social activity dating back to prehistoric people huddling around a fire. Perhaps the origins of the barbecue can be traced back to those ancient days? Slow-cooking meat on an open flame is one of the most popular and easiest methods of preparing food. Worldwide, cities hold gigantic events in the hopes of being declared the new record-holder for **LARGEST BARBECUE**.

A gigantic group of Australians threw the biggest bash at Warwick Farm Racecourse in Sydney, Australia, on 10 October, 1993. The record attendance at this one-day-only barbecue was 44 158 people! The hungry masses devoured more than 300 000 sausages, 100 000 steaks and 50 000 chicken burgers at the **LARGEST BARBECUE**.

TRIVIA
The **GREATEST QUANTITY OF MEAT CONSUMED AT A BARBECUE** was 22 000 kilograms of chicken, which was cooked and consumed in 8 hours at the Lancaster Sertoma Club Chicken Bar-B-Que, Lancaster, Pennsylvania, on 18 May, 1996.

DID YOU KNOW?
In America, cowboys began barbecuing food in the 1880s on cattle drives in the West.

FASTEST EATER

Your nose becomes more aware of food odours when you're hungry. Imagine having terrible eyesight and living in a dark cave. How would you ever find enough food to survive? Your other senses would have to become highly developed. The star-nosed mole (*Condylura cristata*) lives under these conditions, and its amazing 22-tentacled snout always keeps its stomach full.

Dr Kenneth Catania at Vanderbilt University, Tennessee, studied the feeding habits of the star-nosed mole using a high-speed video recorder. His published findings in February 2005 brought the nosy mammal more attention and a Guinness World Record. Its unusually shaped pink nose is the most sensitive mammal touch organ. This strange-looking snout is five times more sensitive than our fingers, and its flexible feelers aid the **FASTEST EATER** in handling small prey — such as worms, insects and crustaceans. The star-nosed mole can identify, capture and consume meals within 120 to 230 milliseconds!

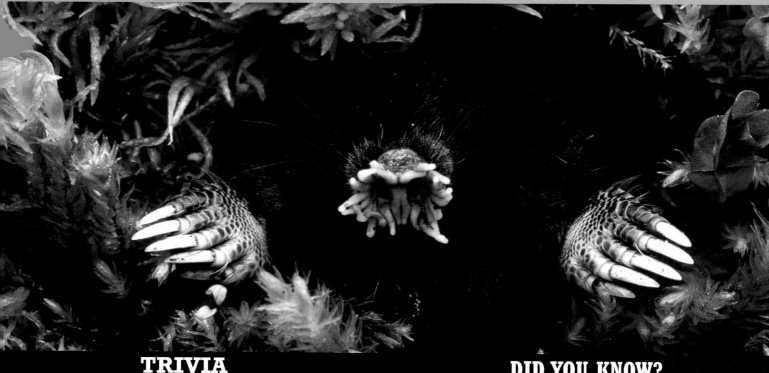

TRIVIA
The star-nosed mole's teeth are perfectly formed for its fast mini-meals. It has tiny incisors, able to grasp small prey as precisely as a pair of tweezers.

DID YOU KNOW?
The star-nosed mole is a semiaquatic mammal, digging homes with its paddle-shaped hands through the marshlands of Canada and the eastern American coastline.

QUIZ ME!

Q. 75
Why is it so important to human beings that an earthworm eats its own weight in food every day?

Q. 76
How many hair cells must an insect trigger in a row before the Venus flytrap springs its 'trap'?

Q. 77
True or False? Michel Lotito, also known as Monsieur Mangetout, was inspired in his metallic dietary choices by a metal-eating goat that was also recognised with a Guinness World Record.

Q. 78
True or False? Heinz® Tomato Ketchup is suitable for diets that are kosher, vegan, vegetarian and gluten-free.

Q. 79
A hamburger is popular around the world — except among cows. How many hamburger patties can be made from an average-size cow?

a) 100
b) 550
c) 720
d) 1001

Q. 80
Calculation check: If everyone ate the same amount, how much would each person have eaten at the **Largest Barbecue** attended by 44 158 people?

Q. 81
What do Eimer's organs have to do with the star-nosed mole?

ANSWERS ARE ON PAGE 141

Test your *Extreme* know-how with these cool quiz questions!

eXTREME SURVI

Many extreme people in this book were either born with or chose to develop their unusual gifts for record-breaking. The survivors in this chapter, however, found themselves in extraordinary **LIFE-THREATENING CIRCUMSTANCES** not of their own choosing. Yet their courage and refusal to give up in the face of such odds is a testament to the sheer tenacity of the human will.

VORS

HIGHEST FALL SURVIVED WITHOUT A PARACHUTE

Vesna Vulović was 23 years old and flying high, literally, in her new job as a flight attendant for Jugoslovenski Aerotransport. Although she had not been scheduled to work on 26 January, 1972, fate placed her aboard Yugoslav Air Flight 364 from Copenhagen, Denmark, to Zagreb, Croatia. A terrorist bomb exploded inside the plane as it flew over Srbská, Kamenice, Czechoslovakia (now Czech Republic). Five crew members and all 22 passengers died as the DC-9 tore apart. Vesna was trapped in the plane's tail section. Sheltering its now-unconscious passenger, the tail plummeted 10 160 metres and crashed into the frozen ground below.

Rescuers combed the countryside despite little hope of finding survivors — instead, they found Vesna, alive and in a coma. Rushed to a hospital in Ceska, Karmenice, Vesna remained unconscious for 27 days while doctors reset her fractured skull, broken vertebrae and broken legs. She awoke, temporarily paralysed, and remained in the hospital for 16 months. Even more miraculously, this record-holder for **HIGHEST FALL SURVIVED WITHOUT A PARACHUTE** made a full recovery, able to walk and travel, with her love of flying undiminished.

TRIVIA

One of Vesna Vulović's rescuers was a former nurse, Bruno Henke, who spotted Vesna among the wreckage. Bruno cleared Vesna's airways and saved her life.

DID YOU KNOW?

The average speed of a skydiver in free fall (parachute closed, limbs extended) is 193 kilometres per hour. A skydiver can achieve a terminal velocity of 320 kilometres per hour by tucking his arms and legs tight against his body.

LONGEST TIME SPENT ADRIFT AT SEA ALONE

A shy young man named Poon Lim from China was the first at-sea survivor. The year was 1942 and World War II raged around the world. Poon wanted to make a difference. He signed up to be the second steward aboard a ship of the British Merchant Navy. He believed it would be a great adventure and make him a more resourceful person — and it truly did. When the S.S. *Ben Lomond* was torpedoed on 23 November, 1942, the crew abandoned ship. Poon jumped into a life raft . . . and suddenly realised he was completely on his own.

Days passed, yet no rescue ship arrived. His limited supplies running low, this increasingly resourceful castaway assembled fishhooks out of nails and flashlight parts. On 5 April, 1943, a Brazilian fishing boat rescued him near Salinópolis, Brazil. Poon walked ashore after a perilous and life-changing journey of 133 days — the **LONGEST TIME SPENT ADRIFT AT SEA ALONE**.

TRIVIA
The S.S. *Ben Lomond* was torpedoed 900 kilometres west of St. Paul's Rocks, off the coast of Brazil.

DID YOU KNOW?
Poon Lim even caught a seabird with his bare hands during his life-raft journey.

LONGEST TIME WITH A BULLET IN HEAD

Never try to re-create this situation! In 1942, Kolyo Tanev Kolev of Bulgaria accidentally shot himself behind his right ear with a pistol. He was only 17 years old. But Kolyo survived. Decades later, he wanted to check on his injury, and the advances made in medical technology allowed him to actually 'see' the bullet in his own head. On 5 July, 2003, X-rays clearly showed the bullet, still lodged at the base of his skull, an amazing 61 years later. Kolyo's initially unfortunate experience and its incredible outcome is the **LONGEST TIME WITH A BULLET IN HEAD**.

TRIVIA

Gunpowder was invented by the Chinese in the eleventh century.

DID YOU KNOW?

X-rays — the ability to take snapshots of skeletons while the person is still alive — was discovered by German physics professor Wilhelm Conrad Roentgen on 8 November, 1895.

HIGHEST G-FORCE ENDURED NONVOLUNTARILY

Astronauts, fighter pilots and Formula One race car drivers are familiar with the effects and forces of velocity upon their bodies and vehicles. Remember the drivers of the Thrust SSC? Every time the jet engine powering that supersonic car was fired up, the drivers experienced a significant change in the g-force pressure. We experience 1 g-force, the pull of gravity upon our bodies, by standing in one place. When we move, the values involved become focused on acceleration and the amount of pressure needed to propel our body mass in a straight line. Turning corners or going in circles increases the amount of g-forces required in completing the manoeuvre.

Racing driver David Purley of the UK survived the **HIGHEST G-FORCE ENDURED NONVOLUNTARILY** on 13 July, 1977. His race car crashed during prequalifying trials for the 1977 British Grand Prix at Silverstone in Northamptonshire, UK. His car, and his body, decelerated from 174 kph to 0 kph within 66 centimetres. This violent change in acceleration rate resulted in 179.8 g-forces crushing against his body mass. David suffered 29 fractures, 3 dislocations, and 6 heart stoppages, and lived to talk about the experience.

TRIVIA
The click beetle (*Athous haemorrhoidalis*) encounters 400 g-forces, the **HIGHEST G-FORCE ENDURED BY AN INSECT**, whenever 'clicking' its body in a jackknife manoeuvre to propel itself 30 centimetres into the air.

DID YOU KNOW?
David Purley was awarded the George Medal for his selfless attempt to rescue another driver, Roger Williamson, trapped in a burning car during the 1973 Dutch Grand Prix.

LONGEST TIME SURVIVED WITHOUT A PULSE

Julie Mills of Surrey, UK, was in her early twenties when she began experiencing chest pains. She thought it was muscle strain and didn't realise the most important muscle in her body was in severe trouble. A few hours later, she was in an emergency room and diagnosed with a rare, life-threatening condition called viral myocarditis. Her heart muscle was inflamed, and because it was gradually failing, her other organs were shutting down.

Doctors and patient wouldn't give up the fight. Julie was transferred to the John Radcliffe Hospital in Oxford, UK. Cardiac surgeons told her of a brand-new procedure not yet performed in the UK: for one week, an artificial heart would handle her heart's regular work while the muscle rested and repaired itself. For three days, Julie was without a pulse in her vascular system, and endured the **LONGEST TIME SURVIVED WITHOUT A PULSE** starting 14 August, 1998. During this time, a nonpulsatile blood pump (AB180) supported her body's functions. Her normal heart recovered, the pump was removed, and Julie reinvigorated her life by volunteering for the organisation CRY (Cardiac Risk in the Young). She helps support other people who, under the age of 35, have to deal with heart problems and the possibility of surgery.

LONGEST SURVIVAL WITH HEART OUTSIDE BODY

In medical terms, *ectopia* means an internal organ develops in a wrong location. Most of these situations occur during pregnancy as a birth defect and greatly decrease the child's chance of survival. Normally, the heart grows beneath the breastbone on the inside of the body. *Ectopia cordis* refers to the displacement of the heart organ. This condition results in the heart protruding from a gap in the chest, abdominal or neck area. This is a birth defect with tragic outcomes for the family. Most patients do not live beyond 48 hours.

Christopher Wall of Philadelphia, Pennsylvania, was born with *ectopia cordis* on 19 August, 1975. However, he is still living today with his condition and is experiencing the **LONGEST SURVIVAL WITH HEART OUTSIDE BODY**.

TRIVIA

Six months after leaving the hospital, Julie Mills flew to the Pittsburgh manufacturing plant of the artificial heart to personally thank its creators for helping save her life.

DID YOU KNOW?

The size of a child's heart is about the same size as their fist. The size of an adult's heart is twice the size of their fist.

QUIZ ME!

Q. 82
True or False? Because of proper training and safety measures, skydiving fatalities are rare.

Q. 83
Poon Lim survived the **Longest Time Adrift at Sea Alone**. What recent popular novel also features a young man adrift on a raft after his ship sinks?

Q. 84
Accidentally shooting yourself in the head is a serious trauma, and Kolyo Tanev Kolev is lucky to have lived. What industrialised country currently has the highest firearms death rate due to accidental shootings?

a) The United Kingdom
b) Canada
c) The United States of America
d) Japan

Q. 85
By standing still, you are experiencing 1 g-force. If you were orbiting Earth in space, what amount of g-forces would you experience?

Q. 86
Amazingly, Julie Mills survived three days without a pulse in her vascular system. At what age do people generally have the highest pulse rate?

Q. 87
True or False? The *ectopia cordis* that Christopher Wall was born with is more common than you would think.

ANSWERS ARE ON PAGE 141

Test your *Extreme* know-how with these cool quiz questions!

EXTREME-ISTS

Every animal, plant, insect, tree and human being is unique in its form, actions and experiences. Record-breaking is all about going beyond the expected. Since humans walk across the ground on foot, why not walk on your hands underwater? You would be surprised at your own abilities and might even invent a brand-new category. Such were the achievements of these record-holders on **EXTREME QUESTS** *of personal excellence!*

MOST PROLIFIC

If there is one person in the entire world *guaranteed* to have a record featured in the yearly edition from Guinness World Records, then it is Ashrita Furman. This is the man who knows how to set and break records — around the world, underwater or atop his chin, multiple and simultaneous, in categories not even thought about before he made his attempt. He is the **MOST PROLIFIC RECORD-BREAKER**, with more than 100 records set or broken, and the holder of 38 current records . . . and he's still going strong!

Ashrita looks like an average 50-year-old man living in Jamaica, New York. But beneath his everyday exterior beats the heart of a strong-willed, imaginative competitor who holds the **MOST INDIVIDUAL RECORDS** and has set a different record on every continent!

Although he says he was never good at sports in school, he has managed to travel up Canada's CN Tower on a pogo stick. He began training and improving upon his body's endurance levels during meditation studies with Indian holy man Sri Chinmoy. His teacher inspired Ashrita to compete against himself in achieving his highest potential. In 2006, he hopped on one foot for 1.6 kilometres in 27 minutes and 51 seconds.

DID YOU KNOW?
Ashrita Furman keeps this in mind during his record attempts:
'Guinness World Records says to me you can do anything if you try.'

RECORD-BREAKER

This most recent attempt was during a visit to Malaysia, one of many countries Ashrita has seen on his record-setting journey. For his next attempt, Ashrita plans on re-breaking some of his own records — including an underwater juggling marathon that was interrupted by a curious shark!

TRIVIA
Food for thought: Ashrita Furman manages a health-food store.

GREATEST WEIGHT BALANCED ON THE HEAD

Many jobs in life help prepare us for future situations. Often, we discover our talents while performing a simple task, such as moving a stack of bricks from the left side to the right side of a construction site. Professional head-balancer John Evans didn't know — at age 18 and carrying those bricks — that years from then he would be touring the globe, delighting thousands of people from different cultures with his unique talents. But what he *did* know in that precise moment was if he could carry double the amount of bricks, then he would save time and earn more money. He discovered his talent for head-balancing when he placed a stack of bricks atop a special hat, called a 'hod', and began walking . . . slowly and carefully, from one end of that construction site to the other. During this now-legendary moment, John stepped across the line between ordinary person and extraordinary record-breaker.

John could stack all 10 of the Guinness World Records he currently holds in 11 categories and balance them atop his head — but paper, even framed, is too lightweight for him. Instead, he balanced 62 *Guinness World Records* books in a 1.85 metre column. A solidly built man at a height of 1.85 metres and weight of 155 kilograms, his strength resides in his 60-centimetre thick neck. John has kept milk crates, footballs, books, and even a car aloft, but the **GREATEST WEIGHT BALANCED ON THE HEAD** involved those old familiar building blocks! On 24 December, 1997, he balanced 101 bricks totalling a weight of 190 kilograms for 10 seconds. The event occurred at the BBC Television Centre in London.

People willingly climb inside boats or onto chairs to be lifted into the air by John. He managed a record load of eager fans, balancing (individually) 92 people on his head for at least 10 seconds each over the course of one hour. On 23 July, 2000 at the Lowestoft Motorcycle Show in Lowestoft, UK, John set the record for **HEAVIEST COMBINED WEIGHT BALANCED ON THE HEAD IN ONE HOUR**. In the 60-minute span, a whopping total weight of 5190 kilograms moved onto and off John's sturdy skull!

TRIVIA

John Evans brings his audience-pleasing talents to charity events around the world. Today, it is estimated he has helped raise more than $1 000 000 for the benefit of others. Now, that's a guy who really uses his head!

DID YOU KNOW?

The Mini Cooper car balanced by John Evans didn't have passengers or an engine, but its 160 kilograms still could have crushed him if he had slipped.

HEAVIEST AIRCRAFT PULLED BY AN INDIVIDUAL

Australian David Huxley would not object to being called a 'plane' kind of guy. This strongman extraordinaire taxied planes down the runway using only his body, a rope, and a towing harness strapped around his shoulders, waist and legs. Plane-pulling since 1991, David worked his way through a fleet of aircraft. By the age of 39, he had pulled, *individually*, different models of the Boeing 747 series to the Concorde.

The **HEAVIEST AIRCRAFT PULLED BY AN INDIVIDUAL** was a Boeing 747-400. The plane weighed 187 tonnes. David hauled it a total distance of 91 metres in 1 minute and 27.7 seconds. This amazing feat of strength happened on 15 October, 1997, in Sydney, Australia.

David's four-month fitness regime prior to a pulling event was only part of his successful formula. His self-confidence and focus helped him imagine that the vehicle was merely an extension of his body and he needed to move it!

TRIVIA

Today, David Huxley applies his talents to pushing and inspiring others in achieving their own goals. He founded the Australian-based Tartan Warriors, an event-management and public-relations company specialising in the promotion of strength competitions.

DID YOU KNOW?

David Huxley didn't use his teeth when tugging a ship loaded with 175 cars *plus* people for 7 metres in Rostock, Germany. The **HEAVIEST BOAT PULLED** was the *Delphin* at 2 217 847 pounds on 19 November, 1998.

MOST FLEXIBLE MAN

Can you touch your toes without bending your knees? How about a back bend or a leg split? These acrobatic skills are used by gymnasts and circus performers. Some people are born more flexible than others, but none more so than the **MOST FLEXIBLE MAN**.

Daniel Browning Smith, USA, aka 'Rubber Boy', represents the ultimate in double-jointed flexibility, as he is able to turn his torso 180° and dislocate both arms and legs. As well as holding the current Guinness World Record for entering a locked strait-jacket in the fastest time (2 minutes and 8 seconds), he can squeeze his body through a tennis racket (25.5 cm at its narrowest) in just 15 seconds, and contort himself into a 68-litre box—that is a space measuring just 34.2 x 40.6 x 49.5 cm!

TRIVIA
Enterology is the practice of squeezing one's body inside a container much too small for it to fit comfortably.

DID YOU KNOW?
Contortion is an ancient form of yoga. Practioners of yoga are known as *yogis*. A man is a *yogi* and a woman is a *yogini*.

STRETCHIEST SKIN

Ehlers-Danlos Syndrome is a rare medical condition affecting the connective tissues, elasticity of the skin, and mobility of the joints. The skin's collagen becomes defective, resulting in a loosening of the skin. Some contortion artists are afflicted with this disorder and turn it into a performance advantage. Another two-time record-holder living with this condition relies upon his skin's enhanced elasticity to help him reach beyond previously set category limits.

On 29 October, 1999, Garry Turner of Caistor, UK, proved he has the **STRETCHIEST SKIN**. The studio and viewing audiences of *Guinness World Records: Primetime* taped in Los Angeles, California, witnessed Garry stretch the skin of his stomach to an incredible length of 16 centimetres.

The temporary discomfort caused during his record attempts is not enough to deter Garry from sharing his famous record of **MOST CLOTHESPINS CLIPPED ON A FACE**. On 27 November, 2004, Garry attached a total of 159 ordinary wooden clothespins to every available inch of his face skin during the Guinness World Records 2005 Roadshow at the Trafford Centre, Manchester, UK. This demonstration eclipsed his previous record of 154 clothespins!

TRIVIA

Garry Turner's favourite trick is to stretch the skin of his neck over his mouth to create the 'human turtleneck'. He demonstrated his skills to passers-by on London's Millennium Bridge in celebration of Guinness World Records' 50th anniversary.

DID YOU KNOW?

Inventor David M. Smith of Springfield, Vermont, patented the first spring clothespin in 1853. The Shakers are credited with the invention of the original wooden clothespeg during the 1800s.

FULL BODY ICE CONTACT ENDURANCE

Wim Hof of the Netherlands has a warm personality, but operates at a colder body temperature of 35 degrees Celsius — especially when he demonstrates his shiver-inducing skills. Wim holds two Guinness World Records for becoming a human ice cube — standing in an ice-filled transparent tube and swimming beneath arctic waters. He uses yoga and breathing exercises to help his body prepare for the extreme temperature changes. The dangers of frostbite are minimal in comparison with the danger of heart and organ failure. Doctors have been present at all of his attempts, yet Wim has never suffered from any of these conditions.

The record for **FULL BODY ICE CONTACT ENDURANCE** requires the participant to have direct, full-body contact with the ice. On 11 September, 2004, Wim climbed into the tube, wearing only swimming trunks, and stood among the ice cubes for 1 hour and 8 minutes, beating his previous record by 56 seconds. This event occurred on the set of the TV show *Guinness World Records: 50 Years, 50 Records* in London. His second record for **LONGEST SWIM UNDER ICE (BREATH HELD)** was set on 16 March, 2000. He dived into a lake near Kolari, Finland, and swam 57.5 metres beneath a metre of ice, wearing only goggles and swim trunks.

Wim believes his feats of endurance strengthen the connection between mind and body and hopes his accomplishments will help other people realise that they are capable of achieving far more than they may have thought possible.

TRIVIA

Wim Hof wore protective eye goggles during his second ice-swimming attempt because his retinas had frozen during his first attempt. Unable to see, Wim nearly missed the hole cut into the ice for his safe exit from the dangerous waters.

DID YOU KNOW?

Skin temperature depends on air chill factors and the environment. Normal skin temperature is around 33 degrees Celsius.

MOST PEOPLE ABOARD A CAR DRIVEN ON TWO WHEELS

Australian daredevil Lawrence Legend became a multiple Guinness World Record holder by setting two records on one day!

Lawrence achieved his record **MOST PEOPLE ABOARD A CAR DRIVEN ON TWO WHEELS**. Legend had eight adults on board, as the daredevil skilfully drove his car on two wheels for a distance of 405 metres. This was a pretty impressive feat, because the weight of 8 people in the car was equivalent to the original weight of the vehicle, therefore doubling its weight! This record was set on 30 July, 2005 in Junee, NSW, Australia for the TV show *Guinness World Records*.

The second record set that day was **SIDE WHEEL DRIVING THROUGH THE SMALLEST GAP** when Lawrence drove his car on two wheels through a space 80 centimetres wider than the height of the car.

TRIVIA
Lawrence is a third-generation stunt performer. Two of his great uncles on his mother's side rode in the Army Motorcycle Stunt Team, and a grandfather on his father's side rode in the globe of death and wall of death.

DID YOU KNOW?
Lawrence Legend grew up in 'Monte Cristo', widely recognised as Australia's Most Haunted House!

QUIZ ME!

Q. 88
Ashrita Furman climbed Canada's CN Tower on a pogo stick. What famous Japanese mountain has he also climbed using a pogo stick?

Q. 89
True or False? In many African societies, women can carry 70 percent of their body weight on their heads.

Q. 90
True or false? David Huxley holds strongman records for pulling planes and lifting boats.

Q. 91
True or False? Double-jointed people like Daniel Browning Smith have more joints than other people.

Q. 92
Garry Turner has Ehlers-Danlos Syndrome, making his skin's collagen defective. Which of the following are also conditions that result from defective collagen?

a) Influenza
b) Acute nasopharyngitis
c) Osteogenesis imperfecta
d) None of the above.

Q. 93
Wim Hof has practised his skill long enough to never suffer from frostbite. Which of the following are warning signs of frostbite?

a) The affected area becomes numb.
b) Skin feels rock hard.
c) Skin appears waxy white, or greyish.
d) All of the above.

Q. 94
True or False? One of Lawrence Legend's first stunts was jumping his bike over a car.

ANSWERS ARE ON PAGE 141

Test your *Extreme* know-how with these cool quiz questions!

BE A RECORD-BREAKER!

MESSAGE FROM THE OFFICIAL KEEPER OF THE RECORDS:

Record-breakers are the ultimate in one way or another – the youngest, the oldest, the tallest, the smallest. So how do you get to be a record-breaker?

FOLLOW THESE IMPORTANT STEPS:

1. Before you attempt your record, check with us to make sure your record is suitable and safe. Get your parents' permission. Next, contact one of our officials by using the record application form at **www.guinnessworldrecords.com**.

2. Tell us about your idea. Give us as much information as you can, including what the record is, when you want to attempt it, where you'll be doing it, and so on.

a) We will tell you if a record already exists, what safety guidelines you must follow during your attempt to break that record, and what evidence we need as proof that you completed your attempt.

b) If your idea is a brand-new record nobody has set yet, we need to make sure it meets our requirements. If it does, then we'll write official rules specific to that record idea and make sure all attempts are made in the same way.

3. Whether it is a new or existing record, we will send you the guidelines for your selected record. Once you receive these, you can make your attempt at any time. You do not need a Guinness World Record official at your attempt. But you do need to gather evidence. Find out more about the kind of evidence we need to see by visiting our website.

4. Think you've already set or broken a record? Put all of your evidence as specified by the guidelines in an envelope and mail it to us at Guinness World Records.

5. Our officials will investigate your claim fully – a process that can take up to 10 weeks, depending on the number of claims we've received, and how complex your record is.

6. If you're successful, you will receive an official certificate that says you are now a Guinness World Record-holder!

Need more info? Check out **www.guinnessworldrecords.com** for lots more hints and tips and news to inspire you to become a record-breaker. Good luck!

QUIZZED OUT!

EXTREME SKILLS

Q. 1
Answer: 'b', John Montague, 4th Earl of Sandwich. In the eighteenth century, John Montague, 4th Earl of Sandwich, wanted to continue playing cards while eating, so he asked that the meat he had been eating with his bare hands be put between two slices of bread — and from that, we have the sandwich!

Q. 2
Answer: False. The 'World Toe Wrestling Organisation' has tried to qualify for the Olympics, but so far, it has been unsuccessful.

Q. 3
Answer: Surfing began in Hawaii. In 1778, members of Captain Cook's third expedition to the Pacific wrote accounts of seeing islanders surfing. However, surfing is believed to have been practised by native Hawaiians since the fifteenth century.

Q. 4
Answer: Llanwrtyd Wells is called 'The Smallest Town in Britain,' with a population of about 600 people.

Q. 5
Answer: Hydrobikes.

Q. 6
Answer: True. The Winter X Games are currently held in Aspen, Colorado, and officially began in 1997.

Q. 7
Answer: Yes! In 1943, Maria Dickin (the founder of People's Dispensary for Sick Animals, a United Kingdom veterinary charity) set up the 'Dickin Medal' as an award for any animal displaying conspicuous gallantry and devotion to duty while serving with armed forces or civil emergency services. Between 1943 and 1949, PDSA awarded 54 Dickin Medals to 32 pigeons, 18 dogs, 3 horses and 1 cat.

Q. 8
Answer: 'd', All of the above.

Q. 9
Answer: 'd', All of the above. A 'flamingo' is standing up on your seat while doing a wheelie, an 'endo' is applying the front brakes while moving to bring the back tyre off the ground, and a 'wheelie' is using the bike's motor to bring the front tyre off of the ground. Don't try these at home!

EXTREME KILLERS

Q. 10
Answer: Only one. In 2003, a biologist was dragged underwater by a leopard seal while snorkelling near an Antarctic research station.

Q. 11
Answer: True.

Q. 12
Answer: No. In fact, only about 15 percent of all snake species have venom that is harmful or fatal to human beings.

Q. 13
Answer: 'a', 2. The Gila lizard and the Mexican beaded lizard are the only poisonous lizards we currently know about.

Q. 14
Answer: 'd', None of the above. The cassowary is actually a shy bird. It can't fly and its diet consists mainly of fruit.

Q. 15
Answer: 'd', More than 10 000. Amazingly, scientists are always finding new ant species in the world.

Q. 16
Answer: True. By hitching rides on cargo ships in bunches of bananas, this spider truly does wander!

EXTREME DANGER

Q. 17
Answer: The black widow spider. The female black widow often kills and eats the male after mating (hence the spider's name). And the male brown antechini thought they had it rough!

Q. 18
Answer: Indeed. A traditional Japanese verse is: 'Last night he and I ate fugu; today I help carry his coffin'!

Q. 19
Answer: No. Sometimes rattlesnakes give off a warning rattle, and sometimes they don't.

Q. 20
Answer: The International Brotherhood of Magicians, which is the world's largest organisation for magicians, with nearly 15 000 members worldwide.

Q. 21
Answer: True. When carbon dioxide erupted from Lake Nyos on 21 August, 1986, the denser gas spilled into the surrounding valley and suffocated thousands of animals and people.

Q. 22
Answer: 'd', 0. There have been no outbreaks of the Ebola virus in the US.

EXTREME SPEED

Q. 23
Answer: True. Grass is the largest irrigated crop in the US, beating out corn by three times. Good thing those lawn mowers can move so fast!

At the end of each chapter was a challenge of your record-breaking smarts. Check your **ANSWERS** against the real facts listed.

Q. 24
Answer: 'b,' the Murphy Bed. The Murphy Bed is a bed that folds down from a wall. William L. Murphy applied for a patent for this idea 1 April, 1916, and it's been going up and down ever since.

Q. 25
Answer: So far, not a one.

Q. 26
Answer: 'd,' All of the above.

Q. 27
Answer: 'd,' All of the above.

EXTREME ON THE MOVE

Q. 28
Answer: While a sonic boom causes a loud noise that sounds like a clap of thunder, it cannot hurt you.

Q. 29
Answer: The Channel Tunnel, or Chunnel, is a 50-kilometre-long rail tunnel beneath the English Channel that connects France and the UK. A hugely expensive project that saw several false starts, it was finally completed in 1994 and is the second-longest rail tunnel in the world. Of course, you look much cooler crossing the Channel with a water-skier behind you!

Q. 30
Answer: 'b,' 98 percent. Because of the *Shinkai* 6500's maximum depth limitation of 6531 metres, most of the world's ocean floor is open to its exploration.

Q. 31
Answer: Water strider insects easily walk on water. Scientists have found that the strider's legs are covered with fine, water-resistant hairs that keep them afloat.

Q. 32
Answer: Adho Mukha Vrksasana is just the name for a handstand in yoga. Adho Mukha Vrksasana literally means Downward Facing Tree Pose. The next time your sports teacher asks if you can do a handstand, you can tell them you prefer doing the Adho Mukha Vrksasana!

Q. 33
Answer: Since their first use in 1967, the transporters have racked up over 4000 kilometres. About the same distance as a round-trip car ride from the Kennedy Space Centre (in Florida) to New York City!

Q. 34
Answer: True! Skateboarding started in the 1950s, when some surfers got the idea of trying to 'surf the streets' — and the skateboard was born.

EXTREME SOUNDS

Q. 35
Answer: False. A 'black hole' is not a hole in the standard sense of the word, but only a region of outer space.

Q. 36
Answer: True. In China, burping after a meal is often seen as a sign that you've enjoyed your food.

Q. 37
Answer: 'd,' All of the above. You might know somnambulism better as sleepwalking, narcolepsy is falling asleep involuntarily, and bruxism is grinding your teeth when you sleep.

Q. 38
Answer: 'Little Elephant Saddle,' 'Floating down the Pin River,' 'Pin Pia,' 'Bamboolin,' 'Dancing with Prathida,' and 'Kaw-Liga' are just 6 of the 24 tracks (songs) available on their second album, *Elephonic Rhapsodies*.

Q. 39
Answer: VJ. In the early 1980s, music videos became popular and the term 'VJ,' or 'video jockey,' was born.

Q. 40
Answer: Yodelling started in the Swiss Alps. It is believed to have been developed as a form of communication between the high mountain peaks there.

EXTREME SMELLS

Q. 41
Answer: Yes! But don't worry, there has only been one recorded instance of a polar bear killing a human in the US (Alaska). Even so, if you see a polar bear, keep your distance.

Q. 42
Answer: Pheromones are biochemicals secreted from the body that are important in communication between animals of the same species. Scientists have shown that animals use pheromones to communicate alarm, find food, mate, etc.

Q. 43
Answer: Your sense of smell is called 'olfaction'.

Q. 44
Answer: True! 'Corpse flowers' reaching heights of more than 3 metres have been found.

Q. 45
Answer: So long ago, no-one's really sure! Garlic is mentioned in the Bible, ancient Egyptians ate it while building the pyramids, and it shows up in ancient Greek literature.

EXTREME EXTENSIONS

Q. 46
Answer: Some famous polydactyls include: Anne Boleyn, the second wife of Henry VIII, who is said to have had 11 fingers; Liam Gallagher, the lead singer of Oasis, who has 6 toes on each foot; and Antonio Alfonseca, pitcher for the Florida Marlins, who has 6 fingers on each hand and 6 toes on each foot (earning him the nickname 'El Pulpo,' the octopus).

Q. 47
Answer: Yes. Cyrano de Bergerac has been the subject of several films, including a 1950 film starring José Ferrer, a 1990 French-language version starring Gérard Depardieu, and a comedic Hollywood version, *Roxanne*, starring Steve Martin.

Q. 48
Answer: Yes. Your inner ear contains about 30 000 or so tiny hair cells. These hair cells are extremely important because each time there is a vibration of sound, the hair cells move, and, when the hair cells move, they send a signal to your brain telling it that a sound has occurred. These little cells are vital for your hearing.

Q. 49
Answer: 'd,' All of the above. Gandalf, Papa Smurf, and Dumbledore may not have much in common, but they all have beards!

Q. 50
Answer: 'c,' A 'moustachio' is a term for a large moustache.

Q. 51
Answer: *Punctate leukonychia* (a medical term for 'white spots'). Don't worry, it may sound scary, but *punctate leukonychia* is quite common and usually harmless.

Q. 52
Answer: Depictions of pedicure-like services have been found in ancient Egyptian tombs.

Q. 53
Answer: Yes. One such culture is the Masai, a tribe in eastern Africa. Among both Masai men and women, stretched earlobes are considered a sign of beauty.

QUIZZED OUT!

EXTREME TEETH

Q. 54
Answer: True. If you define muscular strength as the ability to exert force on an external object, the masseter is the strongest muscle. However, people sometimes claim the heart is strongest because it does more work over one's lifetime than any other muscle and is almost impossible to fatigue.

Q. 55
Answer: 'd,' All of the above. Halitosis is bad breath, gingivitis is inflammation of the gums, and periodontitis is bacterial infection of the gums. Brush your teeth!

Q. 56
Answer: True. Historically, dental extractions were used to treat a variety of illnesses. During the Middle Ages and through the nineteenth century, 'barbers' would extract teeth with instruments such as the 'dental pelican' (which resembled a pelican's beak) or the 'dental key' (which looked like a door key). Ouch!

Q. 57
Answer: Yes! Sperm whales typically have a life span of 50 to 80 years — quite a long life span considering the average Australian human can expect to live approximately 80 years.

Q. 58
Answer: Not really. Because the giant armadillo eats mainly termites and ants, its teeth are peglike; in fact, the giant armadillo completely lacks incisor or canine teeth.

Q. 59
Answer: Yes. In fact, coconut-harvesting training schools exist for monkeys in southern Thailand. Monkeys are often considered a cost-efficient way of harvesting coconuts.

EXTREME FOOD

Q. 60
Answer: False. It really isn't the best idea to swallow it, but bubblegum won't stay in your stomach for years. It normally takes a few days to pass through your digestive system!

Q. 61
Answer: Two Rivers, Wisconsin, calls itself 'Home of the Ice-Cream Sundae'. Reportedly, in 1881, a tourist visited a local soda fountain and asked for chocolate sauce to be poured over a dish of ice-cream. At the time, this was considered a little bizarre. However, this 'invention' soon caught on and became a huge success. But, just so you know, Evanston, Illinois, and Ithaca, New York, are among the other American cities that claim the ice-cream sundae started in their town.

Q. 62
Answer: Idaho. The state produces about a third of the USA's potatoes. Guess what the state vegetable is? That's right: the potato!

Q. 63
Answer: True. Ginger can serve as a digestive aid for mild stomach upset and is commonly recommended by professional herbalists to help prevent or treat nausea and vomiting. (Just don't eat a whole gingerbread house.)

Q. 64
Answer: Yes. The 1962 Japanese film *King Kong vs. Godzilla* shows the two legendary screen monsters fighting each other.

Q. 65
Answer: 'c,' Taiwan. In 2004, one lawmaker threw her lunch box across the room at another legislator during a disagreement. That legislator retaliated, and soon the room of lawmakers began a full-scale food fight that left tabletops, chairs and the floor littered with rice and chunks of hard-boiled eggs!

EXTREME LUXURIES

Q. 66
Answer: Besides being the **Highest Point in the World** at 8848 metres, Mount Everest is also dangerous to climb. More than 1300 people have climbed Everest, but 179 people have died while attempting to reach its summit!

Q. 67
Answer: Yes. Having a fear of the number 13 is called triskaidekaphobia. (Even the term sounds scary!)

Q. 68
Answer: While there's no fixed rule, longer, more complex comic books are often called graphic novels.

Q. 69
Answer: Currently, either Topps or Upper Deck produces all major league baseball cards.

Q. 70
Answer: 'b,' Tyrant Lizard King. Let's break down the word roots of Tyrannosaurus Rex: *Tyrannos* is Greek for 'tyrant'; the word *sauros* means 'lizard', and *rex* is Latin for 'king'.

Q. 71
Answer: 'a,' Switzerland. At more than 10 kilograms per year, the Swiss consume more chocolate per capita than any other nation. Compare that figure to the 5 kilograms of chocolate consumed per American!

Q. 72
Answer: Check out this Web site: *www.elephantart.com*. This is the

At the end of each chapter was a challenge of your record-breaking smarts.
Check your **ANSWERS** against the real facts listed.

Internet home of the 'Asian Elephant Art & Conservation Project.' Here you can see a selection of art created by elephants from around the world, including the Thai Elephant Conservation Centre.

Q. 73
Answer: 'd', Both 'a' and 'b'. The AIBO® comes close to a real dog — but isn't the real thing!

Q. 74
Answer: False. There are more open seats available to those who can pay the steep 20 million-dollar price tag. Save up!

EXTREME APPETITES

Q. 75
Answer: The earthworm actually eats its way through the soil. The ingested soil is ground up and digested, and the waste deposited behind the worm. This process aerates and mixes the soil, and is considered helpful by gardeners and farmers. Research shows that in about 30 square metres of garden soil, earthworms may bring from 2 to 4.5 kilograms of dirt to the soil surface each year.

Q. 76
Answer: The trigger hairs of a Venus flytrap must be touched twice in quick succession so that non-prey stimuli, such as rain, don't falsely trigger the trap.

Q. 77
Answer: False. Goats eating metal is a myth. In fact, goats are actually quite picky eaters.

Q. 78
Answer: True!

Q. 79
Answer: 'c', 720. A single cow, on average, yields enough hamburger meat to make about 720 quarter-pound hamburger patties!

Q. 80
Answer: On average, one person would have eaten: 6.8 sausages, 2.26 steaks and 1.13 chicken burgers!

Q. 81
Answer: The star-nosed mole can eat because of the circle of 22 fleshy tentacles at the end of its snout, which are used to identify food by touch. The incredibly sensitive nasal tentacles are covered with thousands of minute touch receptors known as Eimer's organs, first described by German zoologist Theodor Eimer.

EXTREME SURVIVORS

Q. 82
Answer: True. Despite the seeming danger of leaping out of a plane, fatalities are rare. About 30 skydivers are killed each year in the US, which works out to approximately one death out of every 100 000 jumps.

Q. 83
Answer: In Yann Martel's **Life of Pi**, an unusual young man, Pi Patel, survives on a raft with a Bengal tiger for 227 days.

Q. 84
Answer: 'c', The United States of America.

Q. 85
Answer: 0 g-force. There's no gravity in space.

Q. 86
Answer: Generally, pulse rates are higher in younger people. For example, a resting heart rate for an infant is as high as, or higher than, an adult's pulse rate while doing strenuous exercise.

Q. 87
Answer: False. **Ectopia cordis** is quite rare, occurring from 5.5 to 7.9 times per 1 000 000 live births.

EXTREME-ISTS

Q. 88
Answer: Mt. Fuji, Japan's highest mountain.

Q. 89
Answer: True. In many African societies, particularly where there is no running water, women must carry buckets of water on their heads for their family's cooking, washing and drinking. Scientists are currently studying why these women are able to carry so much with little to no additional expenditure of energy.

Q. 90
Answer: False. David Huxley holds two records in the vehicle-pulling (not lifting!) category.

Q. 91
Answer: False. Every fully formed person has exactly the same number of joints. 'Double-jointed' people can just bend much farther than one might think a joint would allow a limb to bend.

Q. 92
Answer: 'c', **Osteogenesis imperfecta**. You may know influenza better as the flu, and acute nasopharyngitis is just another name for the common cold. However, osteogenesis imperfecta is brittle bone disease and results from having less collagen than is normal. With brittle bone disease, people suffer from weak, fragile bones.

Q. 93
Answer: 'd', All of the above. If you've been playing outside in the cold and you start feeling this way, it may be the first stage of frostbite, called 'frostnip', so get inside!

Q. 94
Answer: True. Lawrence has been stunt riding for many years and made his first leap over his mother's car!

CONCLUSION

Our trip together through the archives of **GUINNESS WORLD RECORDS** is at an end for this collection of extreme stories and statistics. Except your journey doesn't have to stop here! You can read about the experiences and see eye-popping photos of record-breakers in even more outrageous, phenomenal, and extraordinary categories in the annual edition of *Guinness World Records* or at the official online archives (*www.guinnessworld records.com*).

This book and its exceptional people may have inspired you to become a record-holder. Check out the official rules for making a record attempt listed in the back of the book.

We wish you good luck and always remember — every day gives you a new opportunity to do something out of the ordinary and become a record-breaker in your wonderfully unique style!

PHOTO CREDITS

The publisher would like to thank the following for their kind permission to use their photographs in this book: